SERMONS ON OLD TESTAMENT HEROES

SERMONS ON OLD TESTAMENT HEROES

BY
CLARENCE EDWARD MACARTNEY

BAKER BOOK HOUSE
Grand Rapids, Michigan

ISBN: 0-8010-6019-2

PHOTOLITHOPRINTED BY CUSHING - MALLOY, INC.
ANN ARBOR, MICHIGAN, UNITED STATES OF AMERICA
1977

Foreword

THE revival of biography
is an interesting characteristic of the popular literature of the day. Biography has become one of the
chief themes of books, magazines, and even news-
papers. The preacher would do well to note this revival and take advantage of it, for in the Old Testament we have the richest of biographical material.
"Great men," said a great biographer, Thomas Carlyle, "are the inspired texts of the book of history."
Nowhere is this so strikingly true as in the inspired
history of the Old Testament. Around the great
characters of the Old Testament, such as Noah,
Abraham, Joseph, Moses, Samuel, David, and Isaiah,
gather the principal truths and facts in the history
of revelation and redemption.

With a few omissions, such as Job, Solomon, and
Jeremiah, the major characters of the Old Testament
are taken up in the sermons of this volume. Not all
of them, perhaps, are heroes, in the popular sense of
the word; but all are conspicuous personalities, and
all proclaim and illustrate timeless lessons of morality
and life. As we follow the history of these men, and
behold them in their moments of weakness and
sin, or in their moments of courage and magnificent
faith, and as we hear their sighs and groans or listen

to their songs of triumph, what we are hearing is the great and deep music of human life. Deep calleth unto deep.

Preachers and teachers are often on the hunt for suitable and timely illustrations. But what field is comparable to that of Old Testament biography? Whether it is the struggle of two natures, as in Jacob; or the infinite pathos of life's trials, as in the case of Joseph; or the conflict between the desires of the higher and lower nature, as in Balaam; or the reaction of hate and revenge, as in Haman; or the tragedy of great gifts wasted, as in Samson and Saul; or the beauty of penitence and the glory of forgiveness, as in the case of David—where else can we go for such powerful and beautiful illustrations?

Here, too, in the lives of these Old Testament heroes, we can mark the preparation of the world for the Gospel of redemption from sin. Let no one imagine that when he preaches on the characters of the Old Testament he must confine himself to the lower plane of ethics and morality. By no means. What better foil could there be for the display of the jewels of the Gospel than the history of Noah, Abraham, Jacob, Joseph, Moses, David, or Isaiah?

These sermons were preached at morning and evening services in the First Presbyterian Church of Pittsburgh, and are recorded here in the general form in which they were preached.

CLARENCE EDWARD MACARTNEY

Contents

I. *Noah—The man who saved the human race*

AFTER Jonah, Noah is
perhaps the best known character of the Bible. The
reason for this is that his name is associated with the
greatest catastrophe in the history of the human race.
The flood made Noah immortal. Christian faith has
found in his experience an allegory and illustration
of salvation through the Church of Christ. On the
walls of the catacombs, where the first and persecuted
believers at Rome put away their dead in the hope of
the resurrection, pictures of the ark floating on the
abyss vie in number with pictures of Jonah and his
escape from the monster of the deep. In the providence of God, Noah saved the human race from ex-
tinction. We must rank him first, therefore, among
the saviors of mankind. Sad, then, his shipwreck.

Noah appears in a day when the world was sunken
in iniquity. God saw that the wickedness of man
was great in the earth, and that every imagination
of the thoughts of his heart was only evil continually.

[9]

The Bible always deals with the source of things, and in describing the wickedness of that age it does not mention particular acts of transgression, but says that the heart of man everywhere was poisoned and corrupt. A result of this corruption was great violence. Violence is always the accompaniment of, or sequel to, moral corruption and spiritual decline. The crimes of violence which at present amaze and shock us in America, and give us a criminal record beyond that of any nation on the face of the earth, undoubtedly have a definite connection with the lack of faith and the forgetting of God by so many thousands of our people. We can expect worse and darker things, unless a revival of religion shall check the decline from faith and worship.

In the midst of this universal wickedness, there was one man who lived a godly life. Noah found grace with God. It is always hard to live a godly and righteous life. In some respects, I believe it is more difficult to be a Christian today than ever before. One standard after another has been torn down; principles are changed; to many nothing is wrong, and the only consideration is, Is it profitable? that is, profitable in the sense of the present, the animal, and the temporal. One of our magazines recently carried a letter to the editor from a high school boy who said he had been taught by his parents and by his Sunday school that it was right and profitable to be honest. He had his doubts about it, and cited a number of instances in which he thought that honesty had not paid. If anyone could persuade him that honesty was profitable, and would bring in money, he was willing to be honest. That attitude is characteristic of much of the thinking and living of our day. There is a strong ebb tide carrying men away from the fundamental principles of righteousness. Therefore, those who stand for the right because it is right and the truth because it is the truth, and who live their lives according to principle, will find the society and the world of our age increasingly difficult. Against the wickedness of his age, Noah registered the protest of a godly life and a godly home. The world must be preserved and saved over and over again; and God saves it through the individual and through the family, the home. These are the real fountains of life.

God's fiat goes forth for the destruction of the world. There was nothing abrupt or sudden in that pronouncement of doom. God's judgments always come after his mercies and follow the pleadings of his Holy Spirit. When he said, "My spirit shall not always strive with man," he declares not only the limits of his mercy, but the gracious fact of his mercy. God had been patient with the sin and degradation of man. But repentance had not come, and now the hour has struck for God to intervene. He does that in history, in the lives of peoples and of nations, and he does it in the lives of men and women.

The hour comes when the pleading and the warning of God gives way to his righteous judgments.

Noah was commanded to build an ark in order that he may save himself, and others who are willing to be saved from the great flood which was to come upon the earth. In the prompt obedience of Noah we have one of the greatest examples of faith recorded in the Bible. Ages afterward it is not forgotten, for the inspired writer who built with his pen the world's greatest hall of fame, the heroes of faith in the eleventh chapter of the letter to the Hebrews, says of Noah, "By faith Noah, being warned of God of things not seen as yet, moved with fear, prepared an ark to the saving of his house; by the which he condemned the world, and became heir of the righteousness which is by faith."

In what he did, Noah followed faithfully the directions given him by God. He did not make any suggestions to God as to improvements on the ark or how better the world might be saved. He did as God commanded him. God has made clear to the world his plan to save mankind through the Cross of his Son Jesus Christ. Yet man often acts as if he were the savior, instead of the one who is lost and needs to be saved. The real secret of the religious discussions which trouble the Church and the world today and the reason for a falling away from the grand truths of redemption is nothing else than man's unwillingness to be saved in the way God says he must be saved. God sends Christ to redeem us and tells us this is the only Name given under heaven among men whereby we must be saved. Without the shedding of blood there is no remission of sins. Yet all the time we hear of men who want to be saved by their characters, or by their knowledge and wisdom, or who think they don't need to be saved at all.

Noah must have been the object of no small amount of ridicule and laughter when he commenced to build his ark. We can imagine the people scoffing at him as he toiled away at his gigantic barge. They scanned the cloudless heavens and asked Noah where he could see the slightest sign of rain, for there was not even a cloud the size of a man's hand. It had not rained for months, perhaps for years. They had a tradition that the leaves of the Garden of Eden had never been wet with dew. Where was the sign of the flood? Ages afterward, Peter remembered that skepticism and ridicule and said, "It will be just the same before the coming of the day of God. Men will say of the coming of Christ, Where is the promise of his coming? for since the fathers fell alseep all things continue as they were from the beginning of the creation." Such an event, men say, is too stupendous; it would violate the faithfulness and continuity of nature. Christ also compared the unbelief of men in connection with this last great event with the unbelief of those who laughed at Noah when he built the ark. "As the days of Noah were," he said, "so shall also the coming of the Son of man be; for as in the days that were before the flood, they were eating and drinking, marrying and giving in marriage, until the day that Noah entered into the ark, and knew not until the flood came and took them all away, so shall also the coming of the Son of man be."

Noah had the courage which can endure being laughed at. He who would live according to the plan of God and be saved according to the plan of God must be ready to endure ridicule. Even today there is a half-disguised sneer toward those who hold to the simple, but grand, doctrines of the Bible and the way of salvation. Not a few are frightened out of their faith. They laughed at Noah when he was building the ark; but no one laughed at him when the floods came and the earth rolled back to its original watery chaos.

Noah was a preacher of righteousness. He was not willing to be saved alone, but wanted to save as many others as possible. His pulpit was the dock-yard where he built the ark, and his voice was the ring of his hammer as he smote away day after day, week after week, month after month. The trouble with so many Christians today is that they are not preachers of righteousness, either in their own life or in their effort to bring others into the Church. A wave of indifference has engulfed the Church; yet the need was never greater. On the bulletin of a

church sometime ago, I saw this topic announced:
"A World without Hope, and a Church without
Heart." The world has no hope without Christ, for
without Christ it is without God and without hope;
and a Church without heart, without courage, without the conviction that it has the message which is
the hope and the only hope of the world, and therefore does not care whether the world hears that message or not, is a Church whose candle will be put out.

In one sense of the word, Noah was not a successful preacher. The best he could do was to save seven,
besides himself, of the whole race of mankind. Only
seven! And yet, in saving those seven he saved the
world. Faithful preaching, that is, the preaching of
righteousness, which includes the preaching of sin
and repentance and the way of salvation through
Christ will never be without results. The world may
not think much of the results, but God does, for they
are the results which he has appointed and ordained.

When the ark was finished, Noah went into it with
his family, and God "shut him in." Noah must have
been reluctant to see the doors close, for the closing
of those doors meant the passing of the last hope for
the rest of mankind. Yet it was God who closed the
doors. God assumed that responsibility, not Noah.
Sometimes we trouble ourselves unduly over the great
acts of God's government for which he alone is responsible. Shall not the Judge of all the earth do
right?

Now comes the forty days' rain, and after that the flood. "The windows of heaven were opened, and the fountains of the great deep were broken up."

You can make of it what you please; but it is interesting to note that, with the exception of the black race, all races have their tradition of a disaster which overtook the human family through a flood of waters. Babylonian, Greek, Indian, Mexican, Egyptian, all agree to that. God has no mightier, no more terrifying, no more appalling instrument of judgment than a flood of great waters. If you have any doubt as to that, ask the people of Pittsburgh who were there at the time of the Johnstown flood in 1888, when ten thousand persons perished in the angry, swirling, seething flood of waters. But who shall describe this greatest of disasters, this most terrible of all floods? Doré has given us his pictures, which, once seen in childhood, can never be forgotten. The anguish and woe of perishing men and beasts he describes with terrific and appalling power. Poets and orators have followed in his steps. But the thing is too vast, too great, too awful, for words to describe. We leave it just as the Bible leaves it: "The waters prevailed exceedingly upon the earth, and all the high hills that were under the whole heaven, were covered, and the mountains were covered, and all flesh died that moved upon the earth, both of fowl and of cattle, and of beast, and of every creeping thing that creepeth upon the earth, and every man, all in whose nostrils was the breath of life, and all that was in the dry land died." Death! death! death! universal death. Only Noah and his family remained alive. But God remembered Noah.

When the one hundred and fifty days of the deluge were over, Noah, anxious to know the state of the world, sent forth first the raven. The unclean bird, feeding on carrion, did not return unto him. Then Noah sent forth a dove; but the dove found no rest for the sole of her foot and returned unto him in the ark. Then Noah sent the dove out a second time, and when she came back in the evening there was an olive leaf in her mouth. That let him know that the flood was over. Noah was an example in persistence and perseverance. He did not stop when the raven returned not, nor when the dove came back the first time, but persisted in his effort, sending out these spies one after the other until the answer came from God. Most of us get discouraged too easily. A few efforts in prayer, at reading the Bible, and getting at the heart of the Christian message in entering into the spirit of worship in the church, and then we give it up.

Now that the flood was over, the world was making a new start, and that new start is commemorated by the building of an altar. "And Noah builded an altar unto the Lord." "The earth which had been corrupt before God and had perished in his judgments is now rededicated to God by an altar of sacrifice and of prayer. God accepts this token and makes a covenant with Noah. The great disaster will not be repeated. The human family can go forth now to sow and to reap in the confidence that the processes of nature will not be interrupted. "While the earth remaineth, seed time and harvest, and cold and heat, and summer and winter, and day and night, shall not cease." Nor have they ceased to this day; nor will they cease until God's purposes with man in this world are finished and the world comes to an end.

The sign and seal of the covenant was the tender and beautiful rainbow. The rainbow is the most beautiful thing in nature. How soft, mysterious, beautiful, and sublime is that arch which it builds across the sky, touching the earth as if to unite earth with heaven. But the rainbow came after the flood and the rains and the cloud. You do not see a rainbow on a cloudless, rainless day. You see the rainbow when there are clouds and rain. So the most beautiful and most valuable experiences of your life will not be in the day of the unclouded sky and the serene sunlight, but in the days of adversity and of sorrow and trial. Then God's greatest and most gracious truths proclaim themselves across the firmament of our life.

> "I trace the rainbow through the rain,
> And feel the promise is not vain,
> That life shall tearless be."

I wish we could stop here with Noah. I wish that we could leave him bowing with his family at that first altar of the new earth and gazing in rapture upon the tender glory of the rainbow across the heavens. But the Bible does not stop there; neither can I. The Bible does not spare its greatest heroes. "The fairest copy man ever wrote since the Fall has its blots and false strokes." In the day of his prosperity and great success Noah fell into sin. How often that happens. Lot was vexed with the ungodly life of Sodom and was a preacher of righteousness to the inhabitants of that wicked city. But he passes from the stage of history in a scene of drunkenness and debauchery. It was when David had become king, and all power was given into his hands, that he plunged into murder and adultery. It was when Hezekiah had been delivered from the Assyrians and raised up from a bed of sickness that he fell through pride. It was when King Uzziah was at the height of his splendor and power, "when he was strong," that his heart was exalted against God. Alas, who can count on human nature! Here was Noah, who had testified against a whole world, and had endured the persecution and ridicule of the world; yet now, after his great witness and his great deliverance by the hand of God with whom he had found grace, drinking himself drunk and lying senseless and exposed on the earth in the presence of his sons. If after what he had done and what he had seen, and the grand record he had made, Noah fell so low, then who will boast of his safety? Here is the greatest preacher of righteousness that the world has even seen, and now we behold him a castaway and a shipwreck. "Let not him that girdeth on his harness boast himself as he that layeth it aside." "Let him that thinketh he standeth take heed lest he fall."

> "The gray-haired saint may fall at last,
> The surest guide a wanderer prove.
> Death only binds us fast
> To that bright shore of love."

The covenant that God made with Noah was sealed with a rainbow. The covenant he has made with you is sealed with the blood of Jesus Christ, our Savior. Are you under the covenant? John saw a rainbow round about the throne of God. We take that to mean that the judgments of God are for the sinner canceled by the mercy of God. There is a rainbow of God's mercy round about the throne of his justice. Are you under the covenant? Are you trusting in that mercy of God? And is the throne of God before which you stand a throne about which there is no rainbow of mercy and forgiveness? God said to Noah, "Come thou and all thy house into the ark." He still says that today. "Come into the ark." "Look unto me, all ends of the earth, and be saved." "The Spirit and the Bride say, Come. And let him that heareth say, Come. And whosoever will, let him come and take of the water of life freely."

"He trusted in the Lord God of Israel; so
that after him was none like him among
all the kings of Judah, nor any that were
before him."   II KINGS 18: 5.

II. *Hezekiah—Israel's great-est king*

THIS is the inspired ver-
dict on the life and reign of King Hezekiah. "There
was none like him among the kings of Judah." Uzziah
was greater as a conqueror; Solomon was greater in
wisdom; David greater in genius, and in the length,
breadth, depth, and height of human nature: but
none trusted in the Lord God and followed him as
faithfully as did Hezekiah. The gross faults which
stained the lives of the three great kings, David,
Solomon, and Uzziah, are missing in the life of Hezekiah. Since he was human, he had human weaknesses;
but, on the whole, his heart was right with God. His
name means, "God is might," and that was the motto
of his public and private life.

Hezekiah was a great king and ruler, a great or-
ganizer, a great reformer, a great engineer, for he
conducted water by tunnels into the city; a great
patron of literature, for he collected the Proverbs
of Solomon, and perhaps to that labor we owe our

knowledge of that great book. But most of all, Hezekiah was a great servant of God.

Hezekiah was the son of Ahaz and the father of Manasseh. That means he was either the son of the worst king that ever reigned and the father of the next worst, or that he was the son of the second worst king and the father of the worst; for between wicked Ahaz, his father, and wicked Manasseh, his son, it is hard to choose. We make much of heredity and environment, and sometimes too much. But here is the case of Hezekiah, who, although he is the son of the worst of kings, does that which is right in the sight of the Lord. You would think, too, that his son would have been a good man. But instead of that, he was the incarnation of wickedness, although at the end of his wicked reign, he did repent and turn unto the Lord. I have heard people quote the proverb, "Train up a child in the way he should go, and when he is old he will not depart from it," with the emphasis on the "*old*," meaning that although a man brought up in the right way may go astray, he has received something by godly parental training which will never forsake him.

As a boy, hearing these chapters read at morning worship, I used to wonder just what it was that made one king do that which was evil in the sight of the Lord and another do that which was right. I cannot answer that question now; and if I should live for a thousand years, I would not be able to answer it.

Only God knows the secrets of the human heart. We cannot tell why one turns in the right direction and another in the wrong direction. But there is no doubt that they do, or that they are responsible for the direction they take. Strange mystery! From the same home, from the same mother's knee, from the same training, one goes out and does that which is right in the sight of the Lord, and another through a long life does that which is evil. John Calvin leaves the world his debtor, bequeathing to it mighty possessions in democratic government, education, and the Reformed faith; whereas his brother Charles was a scapegrace and a villain.

I. THE REFORMS OF HEZEKIAH

Hezekiah came to the throne at twenty-five years of age, and immediately launched out on his great career as a reformer. In his reign we see the singular providence of God and how he ever watches over his cause in the world. The Kingdom was at its lowest ebb. The follies and iniquities of Hezekiah's father had plunged the nation into moral degradation and national vassalage, Judah now paying tribute to the king of Assyria. Ahaz had set up an image of the fierce god of Ammon, Moloch, with the furnace at his feet, outside the wall of Jerusalem at Tophet, and into that furnace he had cast his own son. At the entrance to the court of the Temple were chariots which he had dedicated to the sun, after the manner of the heathen. On the roof of the Temple he had built altars for the worship of the stars and the sun, and within the Temple he had replaced the great altar with an altar modeled after one which had taken his fancy in a heathen temple at Damascus. When a nation, like a man or a woman, starts to go down, it goes down rapidly, and under the baleful influence of Ahaz, Israel was at a low ebb. The thing was brought to a fearful climax when the lights in the temple were extinguished and its doors were closed. Such was the situation when Hezekiah came to the throne. But the nation's extremity was God's opportunity. Just when it seemed that everything great and good in the nation was lost, God sends Hezekiah. When Christianity was corrupt and debased in Europe, God raised up Luther. God always has his chosen one in waiting. Perhaps today, somewhere within the shadow, he has a chosen one to lead our own nation out of its present darkness and degradation.

"Careless seems the great Avenger; history's pages but record
  One death-grapple in the darkness 'twixt old systems and the Word;
  Truth forever on the scaffold, Wrong forever on the throne,
  Yet that scaffold sways the future, and behind the dim unknown,
  Standeth God within the shadow, keeping watch above his own."

Hezekiah lost no time in instituting his reforms. The chronicler says, "The thing was done suddenly." Great things can be done suddenly when there is a great necessity and a great purpose. Hezekiah had the purpose, and was confronted with the necessity. He had the temple doors thrown open and the sacred precincts cleared of the rubbish and filth which had accumulated; he removed and destroyed the altars of Ahaz, lighted the holy lamps again, and even destroyed the brazen serpent, the historic symbol of the deliverance of the people in the days of Moses when they were smitten with serpents for their sins. Through the centuries it had been housed in the Tabernacle and then in the Temple. But veneration was turning into worship. The people were offering incense to a thing of brass, and Hezekiah with daring courage destroyed even this sacred relic. The Temple was opened with a great sin offering as a token of national repentance. The long-omitted Passover was observed again, and to the repentant nation God turned back and showed himself gracious. Prosperity and peace blessed the land.

The reforms of Hezekiah are an illustration of the influence men in high office can exert. Here we have the civil power, the government, placing itself squarely on the side of morality and righteousness. As in the vision of the Apocalypse, the earth helps the woman; the civil government supports religion. Why should it not always be so? Why should we be so skeptical about new parties which are turned into office, about men elected to the highest offices in state or nation? Why do we count so little on their help in the warfare with atheism and infidelity, with immorality and vice in a thousand forms? Because sad experience has taught us that we can put little reliance there. "Put not your trust in princes"; nor in politicians. There are financial and industrial evils and evils under all forms of government. But what are they compared with the sinful practices which all the time make war on the soul of the nation? Just as a President would lead the people against the foe in time of war or invasion, so our presidents, our governors, our mayors, like Hezekiah, ought to lead the people in the war against internal foes and wrongs.

II. HEZEKIAH AS A PATRIOT

We have seen him lead the war against idolatry and irreligion within the state. Now we behold him lead the people in the time of invasion. Rumor has reached Sennacherib in far-off Nineveh of the regeneration and revival of the Hebrew nation, his western vassal; and he comes with his army to put a stop to Hezekiah's pretensions. Hezekiah was both vigorous and faithful in the measures which he took. He turned the country into a wilderness around Jerusalem by stopping the fountains and the wells; and when he had done all that he could he reminded the people that with Sennacherib was "the arm of flesh, but with us the Lord our God."

At first it looked as if Sennacherib had the stronger arm, for after a time Jerusalem was straitly shut up and Hezekiah was compelled to pay tribute for the relief of the city. But as soon as Sennacherib had departed he begins to plan another revolt. Sennacherib marches westward once more, and stops to reduce the stronghold of Lachish. Then, drawn southward by a threat from Egypt, he sends his lieutenant with a blasphemous and insulting letter, demanding the surrender of the city. Hezekiah, who always worked in harmony with the great prophet Isaiah, sent his ministers to inform Isaiah, and then went up to the temple of God, and spread out the blasphemous letter of the Assyrian king before the altar. It was as if he had called upon God to behold and hear how Sennacherib had blasphemed his name, and rise up to vindicate his majesty and his power. What Hezekiah did was no strange thing for him to do. For a long time he had known the way to prayer and to worship. Mark out that path to God's altar today, and when the day of trouble comes it will be easy and natural for you to find your way to God and to his help.

Through Isaiah God sends to Hezekiah the assurance that his prayer is answered, and that God's honor will be vindicated. There are few, if any, passages in the Bible which equal in flaming eloquence Isaiah's denunciation of Sennacherib and his prediction of his overthrow. God will put his hook in his nose and drag him back to Nineveh by the way he came. He will send his blast upon him. It is a

dreadful thing for a man or a nation when God sends
forth his blast upon him. The boasting king of
Nineveh awoke one morning to find more than
185,000 of his soldiers dead. Historians labor hard
to explain what happened—pestilence or hurricane.
The best interpretation is what the record says, "The
angel of the Lord went forth and smote in the camp
of the Assyrians a hundred fourscore and five thousand."

"For the angel of death spread his wings on the blast,
  And breathed in the face of the foe as he passed,
  And the eyes of the sleepers waxed deadly and chill,
  And their hearts but once heaved and forever grew still.

And there lay the steed with his nostril all wide,
  Though through it there rolled not the breath of his pride
  And the tents were all silent, the banners alone,
  The lances unlifted, the trumpets unblown,
  And the might of the Gentile unsmote by the sword,
  Hath melted like snow in the glance of the Lord." [1]

Yes, there are times when God does intervene, and
the whole earth stands still and sees his salvation.
There are other times when he seems to let the heathen
rage. There are times when we think he ought to
intervene when he does not. There are times when
"he hides himself so wondrously as if there were no
God." Yet he intervenes often enough to let us know
that the world order is moral, and that God never

[1] Byron's *Hebrew Melodies.*

[28]

forgets his people or his Church. How near is the shadow to our sunlight.

III. HEZEKIAH IN SICKNESS

Hezekiah was at the height of his power and influence. He was in the midst of his days, thirty-nine years of age. He had regenerated the nation and had seen it delivered from a hostile country. He had great plans and projects for the future. Then, suddenly, Isaiah comes to him with his blunt message: "Set thine house in order; for thou shalt die, and not live." Hezekiah had everything to live for, as the saying goes. The expected and the natural thing for us is that we shall live; and yet death is just as natural. Everyone by virtue of his birth carries with him the announcement of his death. All life is but a sentence to death.

Hezekiah took the announcement of his death much as we might have expected. He turned his face to the wall and prayed to the Lord to prolong his life, reminding him of his obedience and his faith. Men then had a blank outlook on the future life. In the song which he composed after his recovery Hezekiah, almost the most devout man of the Old Testament, draws back from death as the end of all life and hope's annihilation. "The grave cannot praise thee. Death cannot celebrate thee. They that go down into the pit cannot hope for thy truth. I shall not see the Lord even in the land of the living. Mine age is departing and is removed from me as a shepherd's tent." Contrast that with what the Apostle Paul said, "I have fought a good fight; I have kept the faith; I have finished the course. Henceforth, there is laid up for me a crown, which the Lord the righteous Judge will give me at that day," and you begin to understand how true it is that Christ brought life and immortality to light in the Gospel. Hezekiah stands in the shadow; Paul in the light of Christ's revelation and resurrection. Yet, as far as a religious man could go, Hezekiah went. He asked God to spare his life, and before Isaiah was gone far from the palace, he received another message telling him to go back and inform Hezekiah that his life would be prolonged fifteen years. Does God not know his mind? Does he say one thing this hour, and another thing the next? God's decrees are always related to our obedience and to our faith, and whether he lived one day or fifteen years, still it was true what the prophet said, "Thou shalt die and not live."

Hezekiah was so weak and so near to death that Isaiah appreciated what a sign would mean to him at that time. So he pointed to the great dial of Ahaz, probably some heathen pillar that he had set up in the palace courtyard. When the sun was rising the shadow fell to the west, and when it was going down the shadow retreated down the eastern steps. Day by day, lying on his sick bed, Hezekiah had watched the advancing and retreating shadow. Isaiah gave him his choice. Would he have for a sign the shadow of the dial going forward fifteen degrees, or backward? To Hezekiah it seemed the greater miracle that the shadow should go backward, and that was the sign he asked. If God made the sun, I suppose he could send it back on its course; and if he created the life of Isaiah, he certainly could prolong it for fifteen years.

> "Admit a God—that mystery supreme!
> Nothing is marvelous for Him to do;
> Deny Him—all is mystery besides."

Isaiah then took the part not only of a prophet, but of a physician, and prescribed for Hezekiah's carbuncle a poultice of figs. When God wants to heal a man, does he need a poultice? When he wants to raise up a man from a sick bed, does he need a doctor? Could he not have healed Hezekiah with his word, without the figs? Certainly he could have done so. Yet God, who can work immediately if he so wills, often chooses to work through means also. This was a case of faith healing; but faith healing with common sense and such science as was available.

IV. Hezekiah's Fall

We could wish the biography of this noble man had come to a conclusion without this last chapter. Why was he not permitted to pass off the stage of Israel's history without this black mark being registered against him? But the Bible is no respecter of its greatest men. It paints them just as they were. Recovered from his sickness, Hezekiah expressed his gratitude in a song, and in this song he declared his penitence, and how he would walk carefully before God and go softly all his years. By his adversity and suffering he said he had learned great lessons. "O Lord, by these things men live." But Hezekiah did not keep his vows. How easy it is to forget the holy impressions made in some hour of sickness or sorrow or bereavement or danger, and to neglect the vows made at that time. Jacob, assured of God's presence, and comforted with the dream of the ladder down which the angels of God came, set up his stone pillow for a pillar and vowed that if God was with him he would come there and worship again. But it was more than a quarter of a century before Jacob kept his vow.

An embassy appeared in Jerusalem from the ruler of the rising kingdom of Babylon. The embassy brought a message from the king of Babylon congratulating Hezekiah on his recovery from his sickness. Flattered by their coming and their message, Hezekiah showed them through his palaces and his armories and his storehouses, displaying to them all his riches, his silver and his gold, and all the resources of his kingdom. It was, even from a worldly standpoint, a foolish thing to do, for it excited the cupidity of Babylon and advertised the riches of Hezekiah's kingdom. But more than that, it was an

irreligious thing to do. Instead of boasting of his
riches, Hezekiah ought to have told them of the greatness of Jehovah, and how God had delivered the kingdom out of the hand of the Assyrians. As soon as
the embassy had gone their way with their valuable
information, Isaiah appears again and tells the king
that all which he had displayed to the ambassadors
of Babylon would one day be carried off by the armies
of Babylon as spoil. When Solon came to visit
Croesus at Sardis, he warned him against a confidence
in earthly things and a continuance of his prosperity.
"Call no man happy," he said, "till you know the
nature of his death." So Hezekiah is an example of
how a good man may stumble at the very last.

> "The gray-haired saint may fall at last,
>   The surest guide a wanderer prove;
> Death only binds us fast
>   To the bright shore of love."

Thus Hezekiah passes from the stage of Hebrew
history, a stage which he had greatly adorned. He
stumbled toward the end; but the whole course of
his life was Godward and his history shows us how
great a power God can be in our lives if we desire it.
Therefore, seek the Lord. In adversity and trouble,
in sickness and in death, in prosperity and in want,
he says to us, "I am thy God."

"O Daniel, a man greatly beloved."

DANIEL 10: 11.

III. *Daniel—The most influential man of the Old Testament*

DANIEL was a man greatly beloved of God, and greatly admired of men. His life is an epic of moral courage, which alone makes men great. Daniel may be described as the most influential man of the Old Testament, for he has exerted more practical influence upon readers of the Bible, and especially upon young men, than any other Bible character. Nothing better could be recommended to young men than a study of the career of Daniel; and if his life and character were studied and meditated upon by thousands of young men, the shores of time would be strewn with fewer shipwrecks. The power of the influence of Daniel was recognized by his own contemporary, the Prophet Ezekiel. Through him judgment was declared upon Jerusalem, and as a sign of the certainty of that judgment the Lord, through the prophet, says that even if three such men as Noah, Daniel, and Job lived in the land, their presence could not save it from the impending doom. This amounts to saying that if the life and character and presence of any man could save a city from destruction, Daniel's would.

Some Old Testament characters, such as David, teach us not only by their virtues but by their sins, not only by their achievements but by their fall. But Daniel inspires us by his victories over temptation. The gross sins which stained the lives of some of the greatest men in the Old Testament are totally wanting in the life of Daniel. Like Samuel, Daniel is one of the aristocrats of the Old Testament, a thoroughbred in every respect; one of those men who, however born and wherever stationed, bear unmistakable marks of intellectual and moral distinction.

I. DANIEL'S YOUTH

Daniel's early years were passed amid the stormy days of the fall of Jerusalem, when Nebuchadnezzar took the city. The king of Babylon directed his ministers to select a number of choice young men who were to be taken down to Babylon, to be brought up in the king's court where they would learn the lore and language of Chaldea and be fitted for the service of the state. Daniel was one of the young men thus selected for education at Babylon. The qualifications stated by Nebuchadnezzar for these ancient Rhodes scholars were, first of all, physical health and strength; they were to be young men without blemish, bright in intellect, trustworthy in character, and with an ability and a personality which would fit them to serve in the court of Babylon.

In company with three other famous youths, and others besides, Daniel made the long journey from Jerusalem down to Babylon. When they arrived in that brown capital on the yellow Euphrates, the seat of world empire, they experienced for the first time the stir and excitement of a great capital and saw, no doubt, a thousand sights, which repelled them and disgusted them and offended their religious principles. Nebuchadnezzar's chamberlain was instructed to take the young men in charge for three years. He changed their names from Hebrew names to Chaldean, but, as subsequent events were to prove, he was not able to change their principles.

At the king's table Daniel and his companions would be required to eat that which was abhorrent to a Jew, either because it was forbidden meat, like the flesh of swine, or because of the way it had been prepared, or because of the fact that it had been profaned by idolatrous rites at the table. Thus at the very outset a crisis in Daniel's moral life was precipitated. What would he do? It is not difficult to know what many would have done under the same circumstances. Daniel might have said, "When we are in Babylon, we had better do as the Babylonians do." Or, he might have argued to himself about things forbidden by the Jewish law, and justified his conduct on the ground that there is nothing inherently right or wrong in what a man eats or drinks. What comes out of the heart, and not what goes into the body, defiles it. Or, he might have said that at first for a little season he would show no scruples, but later on at a favorable time he would abandon the Babylonian diet. Or, he might have said to himself or to his companions that the pressing of their Jewish peculiarities as to meat and drink might lose for them whatever chance they had for preferment at the court. They would never see Jerusalem again, therefore they might as well conform their lives unto the manner of living in Babylon. Many a young man or young woman would have said so. Many, even today, will say so, not in Babylon, but in our city.

But Daniel said No. He purposed in his heart that he would not defile himself with the king's meat. His mind was made up. Nothing could alter his decision. He did not meet this crisis by parley, by compromise, or by postponing a settlement, but with an immediate and indomitable No. Daniel made the right start. In a race, or in life, or in any new circumstance in life a great deal depends upon the way in which one starts. Daniel started right and kept right to the end. If one in the early years of one's life were to ask the heavenly powers for a gift which would equip one beyond all other gifts to pass successfully and honorably through life, one could not do better than to ask for the ability to say No. Daniel could say No courteously and yet louder, more firm, more im-

pressibly than any man in the Bible. Plutarch tells
of the inhabitants of a country in Asia who came to
be subjects and vassals to another country only because they were not able to pronounce one syllable,
"No." There are still multitudes of people who
become slaves and vassals in life to circumstances and
to passions because they are not able to pronounce
the syllable, "No." Influence upon others is never
won without resisting the influence for evil of others
upon ourselves. The world went wrong in the beginning because its first inhabitants could not say
"No," and it has been going wrong on the same principle ever since.

Daniel's stand for principle marked him here at the
very beginning of his career in Babylon as a man of
moral courage. He contrasts in that respect sharply
with multitudes of Christians in the world today.
Instead of being steadfast and loyal to their Christian inheritance and their citizenship in the heavenly
Jerusalem, as Daniel was to his citizenship in the
earthly Jerusalem, they abandon it and betray it
upon the slightest pressure from the world. They
might be described as chameleons. The chameleon
takes the color of his background and environment—
trees, bush, or sod. Many Christians are chameleon-
like in the facility with which they can take on the
color of the world about them, and just as it is difficult to distinguish the chameleon from the background whose color he has taken, so it would be very

difficult to distinguish many Christians from the background of the world in which they live.

II. DANIEL AS A MAN

Daniel did not lose anything by standing for his principles and by loyalty to his faith. No one ever did. The king of Babylon was looking for men of such character and courage, and Daniel is advanced to a post of honor among the wise men of Nebuchadnezzar's kingdom. Looking at him on this exalted stage, we see very quickly that the boy was father to the man. The same courage that he had displayed in taking a stand concerning the king's meat, he now displays as a seer and a minister of three successive kings—Nebuchadnezzar, Belshazzar, and Darius. It took courage, as well as inspiration, for Daniel to tell Nebuchadnezzar the interpretation of his two dreams: that the dream of the huge colossus with the head of gold and the feet of clay which was crushed and scattered by the unhewn stone meant the destruction of his own kingdom; and it took courage again for him to tell the king that his dream of the mighty tree whose branches reached to heaven and under which the beasts of the field took refuge, but which was hewn down and wet with the dew of heaven, meant that the king himself was to be driven out from the presence of men and to eat grass like the ox. It took courage again for him to interpret the dread handwriting which came out on the wall where the debauched Belshazzar was reveling with a thousand of his drunken lords and their ladies, and to tell him that his kingdom would be taken from him that very night. Daniel spoke as the representative of the King of kings, and therefore he was not afraid to pronounce judgment upon the kings of this earth.

Just as the prophet Nathan said to David, "Thou art the man," so Daniel could say, "Thou!" to the potentates of Babylon. But the greatest exhibition of the courage of Daniel came in the reign of Darius, the Mede and Persian king who had succeeded to the empire of Babylon. One of the first things he did was to elevate Daniel to the rank of one of the three men who were over the one hundred and twenty satraps of that vast realm. "Wrath is cruel and anger is outrageous, but who is able to stand before envy?" Daniel has risen so high that he attracts to himself the arrows of slander and defamation. This is one of the prices which distinction and ability must ever pay.

> "He who climbs the mountain slopes
>   Will find the highest peaks
>   'Most clothed in snow.
>   And he who conquers and subdues mankind
>   Must look down on the hate of men below."

The enemies of Daniel were determined to bring him down. But how to do it, that was the question? Daniel administered the exchequer of the great empire. Possibly they might find some irregularity or peculation in the discharge of his stewardship. But when they looked into the matter they were unable to discover anything which even malice or hate could distort into dishonesty. "He was," it is written, "faithful, neither was there any error or fault found in him." That is the way a man ought to live, so that when his enemies would bring him down they can find no occasion against him. Spurgeon, threatened with blackmail by evil men, who said that if he did not meet their demands they would publish things which would ruin his reputation, answered, saying, "Write all you know about me across the heavens."

These plotters against Daniel knew that it would be impossible to trap him or bribe him into any dishonesty or disloyalty or irregularity. Daniel, they knew, was beyond all that. The only way they could hope to bring him down was to ruin him by his very loyalty to God. Therefore they persuaded Darius to issue a decree that, upon pain of being thrown to the lions, no inhabitant of Babylon was to pray for thirty days to any god but to Darius. Daniel's enemies knew that he was a man of prayer. They knew, too, that he feared God rather than man, and that Daniel would never obey such a decree, and the moment the decree was stamped with the signet ring of the king they said to themselves, "Now we have Daniel in our power."

That very night they went off to the palace of Daniel and stationed themselves near the window. It was Daniel's custom to open his window toward Jerusalem and to pray three times a day and give thanks to God. No doubt, in praying toward Jerusalem as a Moslem today prays toward Mecca, Daniel was not unmindful of what Solomon had said in his prayer at the dedication of the Temple: "What prayer and supplication be made by any man who shall spread forth his hands toward this house, then hear thou in heaven thy dwelling place." Daniel knew his peril and that his enemies would be spying on him. It would have been easy for him to have said to himself, "I can pray in the spirit without going to the window as my custom is. God will hear and observe and answer, just as truly as if I had opened the window toward Jerusalem." But Daniel was the sort of man who felt it was more dangerous not to pray to God as his custom was than to go into a den of lions. As the night wears away, and the blackness turns to gray, and the gray to gold and red, the sun comes out of his chamber rejoicing as a strong man about to run his race, disclosing with his rising beams the tawny Euphrates as it flows through the immense cluster of adobe huts, and past the huge mounds, temples, palaces, and the Hanging Gardens which Nebuchadnezzar had built for his homesick wife. We can imagine one of the plotters and watchers saying to his fellow, "No window has opened as yet. Daniel is not going to pray in open, and our plot is in vain." But his companion answers, "Have patience. The window will open. Nothing will stop Daniel from praying." His companion rejoins, "Yes, but what will a man give for his life? Hark! Do you hear the roar of those lions?" But before the other can answer, the casement is slowly opened, and the aged statesman kneels down and spreads out his hands toward Jerusalem, perhaps making a prayer like that of the captive singer of the Psalms: "If I forget thee, O Jerusalem, let my right hand forget her cunning."

When Daniel's enemies went eagerly back to Darius with their evidence that Daniel had broken the law of the king, Darius, realizing that he had been trapped, was sore distressed; and yet the law of the Medes and the Persians changes not. All that day and all that night food, music, and sleep the king put away from him. His thoughts were upon Daniel in the midst of the wild beasts. Yet he had hope that something would intervene to save the life of Daniel, for when Daniel was bound and led away, the king had said to him, "Thy God, O Daniel, whom thou servest, he will deliver thee." What a tribute that was to Daniel's God, and Daniel's faith in his God. When the crisis arises, when the storm breaks, will our friends be able to say of us in the hour of our deepest distress, "He has a great God who will deliver him"?

In the early morning the king hurries out to the lions' den and, looking down through the grating, cries out, "O Daniel, servant of the living God, is thy

God whom thou servest continually able to deliver thee?" and up from the dark recesses of the den of lions comes Daniel's answer, "O king, live forever. My God hath sent his angel, and hath shut the lions' mouths that they have not hurt me." The old jest that the lions were not able to eat Daniel because he was all backbone has a great deal of truth in it. But there are many who ought to be the inheritors of the faith and courage of Daniel who would fare ill in a den of lions. Even a toothless and decrepit old lion would have little difficulty in devouring them, so boneless a species are they. This was a magnificent climax to the story of Daniel; yet the story would have been just as great if the lions had devoured Daniel, because it would have been the story of a man who gave up his life for the truth, and greater love and greater faith, and greater courage, hath no man than this.

It is a very significant fact that among the books of the Old Testament, it is this book of Daniel which deals with a magnificent exhibition of moral courage, which yet sounds more clearly and triumphantly than any other Old Testament book the great Christian note of resurrection and immortality. "Its messianic note has charmed all mankind by the offer of infinite hope."

Toward the end of his life Daniel, like his great successor on the isle which is called Patmos, was granted an Apocalypse, and in that grand Apocalypse we see nations and empires follow one another in swift succession and go down in ruin with world resounding crash. Daniel himself was overcome by the splendor and terror of what he had been permitted to witness, and inquires about the meaning of the vision and the end and issue of all these things. His curiosity is not answered, but he is given a great assurance. There is declared to him the great truth of the resurrection of the dead, that many of them that sleep in the dust of the earth shall awake, some to everlasting life and some to shame and everlasting contempt. God's Kingdom shall have a glorious victory. Time's drama is God's drama, and the great kingdoms and the great men of the world are but the brief embodiment or the transient realization of the divine purpose. They who are faithful to God endure forever. They that be wise shall shine as the brightness of the firmament, and they that turn many to righteousness as the stars forever and ever. Daniel, who in his day and generation had witnessed so courageously to God, is told that there is a place reserved for him. "Thou shalt rest and stand at thy lot at the end of days." There, then, we leave him, shining as the brightness of the firmament, one of the brightest of those stars which have turned many to righteousness and have pointed men to God and Everlasting Life.

"Now I know that thou fearest God."
GENESIS 22: 12.

IV. *Abraham—The greatest believer and the greatest blessing*

HEBRON is one of the world's oldest towns, and stirring memories of events in the history of Israel gather around it. But the most interesting thing at Hebron is a grave. When Sarah died Abraham went to the children of Heth and asked them to sell him a plot of ground, "that I might bury my dead out of my sight." The ground which they sold him was the cave of Machpelah, and that grave was the only part of the land that had been promised him that Abraham ever owned.

Today the cave of Machpelah is covered by the Mosque of El-Haran. For many centuries no Christian or Jew could enter this mosque. But in recent years it has been thrown open to visitors, to all save Jews, for on the winding stone stairway, roofed over, which leads from the dismal street of Hebron to the mosque, the seventh step marks the limit any Jew may go. Strange irony this, that the Arabs, who are the descendants of Ishmael, the son

[46]

of Abraham's bondwoman, should exclude from the grave of Abraham, the descendants of Isaac, the son of the promise. Within, the mosque, richly decorated by wealthy Moslems, shows every token of veneration and esteem. One sees not the tombs of the patriarchs, but their cenotaphs, huge bake-oven-like structures, higher than a man, and draped with gorgeous brocade, green for the patriarchs and crimson for their wives. The cenotaphs stand behind silver grills. In the floor of the mosque there is an opening covered with an iron grating, from which is suspended a lamp which is never permitted to go out. Peering down through the opening, one sees the burning lamp in the midst of the darkness. That is all; and yet that burning lamp marks one of the most interesting spots on the face of the earth, for there where the lamp is burning sleeps the dust of the three patriarchs, Abraham the friend of God, meek and gentle Isaac, and Jacob, the prince with God. Has all earth such a spot as this? The phrase which comes to your mind as you peer down into the gloom where the dust of the patriarchs lies, and realize that their God is our God, and that God is the God of the living and not the dead, is that oft-repeated saying of the Bible, uttered in great crises and linked with great promises, "the God of Abraham, Isaac, and Jacob." Let us sit down in the cool shadows of this mosque and talk for a little with one of the patriarchs, the friend of God, for when we talk with a friend of God we talk with God.

The faith of Abraham was the fountain whence flowed the stream of faith and religion and the worship of the true God. Our worship today goes back to that original interview which God had with Abraham when he appeared to him in Haran and called him to go out into a land that he knew not. All believers follow in the footsteps of Abraham, because through him comes the inheritance of faith. The promise which God gave him that in him all families of nations should be blessed has been fulfilled. That is true. Through faith Abraham has blessed all nations. He is the most revered figure of history. The Arabs, descendants of his son Ishmael, and Moslems throughout the world venerate him. The Jews look upon him as the founder of their nation, and the Christians honor him as the father of the faithful, a type of saving faith in Christ, for Abraham believed in God, and it was accounted unto him for righteousness. Like a majestic mountain Abraham towers sublime over all other mountains and all other lives. On what side shall we commence to climb this mountain?

I. THE CALL OF ABRAHAM

God appeared to him in Haran where he and his father had stopped on their western migration from Ur of the Chaldees. There Abraham was told to go out from his father's house and from his kindred unto a land which God would show him. This was the beginning of God's plan to bless and redeem the world through a chosen people. It marks one of the great epochs in the history of redemption, and is worthy to take a place by the giving of the Law through Moses, the Covenant with Noah, the birth of Christ, and the bestowal of the Holy Spirit. The work which commenced when God called Abraham will come to an end when Christ shall appear the second time without sin unto salvation.

The first step, therefore, in the work of redemption was the separation of a people. There the great foundation was laid. God called Abraham out from the idolatry and the customs of that Mesopotamian world in which he had been brought up. Separation is the way to spiritual power and service. If a church is to count, if an individual believer is to count, then there must be separation. The Church that is just like the world can do little for the world. The Christian who is no different from the man of the world exerts no influence for the Kingdom of God. We are not to be conformed to this world, but to be separated from it. The present grave crisis in morals and in religion calls for the testimony of separation and dissent. "Ye are the salt of the earth." Salt does its work because it is different from what is about it. But if the salt has lost its savor, it is good for nothing but to be cast out and trodden underfoot of men. "Get thee out! Get thee out!" That word which God spake to Abraham I think I hear today on every wind that blows.

The promise that God gave to Abraham, that in him all the families of the earth were to be blessed, has been fulfilled. Of Abraham came the Jews, and through the Jews the Law and the prophets, and through them and after them Christ and the Church. What God said to Abraham about his descendants, too, the Jews, has been strikingly fulfilled. "I will bless them that bless thee, and curse him that curseth thee." History reiterates that declaration of God. But, one asks, has God favorites? We are not discussing the aspects of God's providential dealings. All that we are doing just now is to read history. Egypt cursed Israel, and where is Egypt today? The pyramids are all that remain of her power. Assyria cursed Israel, and where is Assyria today? Huge mounds where Nineveh lies buried, and here and there a winged bull or lion, that is all that is left of Assyria. Babylon cursed Israel. Where is Babylon today? Only a few heaps of dust by the tawny Euphrates remain of that world empire. Russia cursed the Jews; and in the reign of judgment and agony that came down upon Russia in our own day and generation, Jews were the active spokesmen and leaders. Let present-day persecutors of the Jews beware. The Jew is God's autograph. Like a river, he has flowed through the ocean of humanity, yet never blended with it. Like the burning bush of Moses, the fires have burned him, but not consumed him.

II. THE SIN OF ABRAHAM

Until we come to this sin, everything about Abraham is noble, uplifting, even majestic. Great his faith, great his simple friendship with God. How easily and naturally he talks with God and God with him. It seems to be a picture of that communion with God which was lost when man fell at the beginning of his history. How beautiful the magnanimity and pity of Abraham. He will not strive with the ambitious Lot, his nephew, but lets him choose whatever part of the land he desires. And how wonderful Abraham's intercession for Lot and the cities of the plain, Sodom and Gomorrah; how in his twilight walk with the three men, God manifest, even then, in the Trinity, Abraham, taking his stand on the truth, "Shall not the judge of all the earth do right?" got from God the promise that Sodom would be spared if it could muster first fifty, then forty-five, then forty, then thirty, then twenty, and finally ten righteous men. Abraham, like Christ, when he saw the multitude, was moved with compassion. You can divide people into two classes, those who care and those who do not. The Church today has many things which it must recover, and among those things is that deep concern for the lost, for the salvation of men, which gave spiritual earnestness to our Churches and sent our missionaries throughout the world. We need a baptism of the spirit of Abraham when he interceded for the cities of the plain.

Now we turn the page and come upon this other Abraham, and we are shocked and amazed to discover in him the crafty, cowardly liar of Gerar and Egypt. Alas, with all his grandeur, he is but human, a man of like passions with ourselves.

When he went down into Egypt, and the second time, when he went to the land of Gerar, Abraham, to protect himself from bodily harm, resorted to a cowardly falsehood. Sarah was a beautiful woman, and fearing that the rulers of Egypt and Gerar would covet her, and would kill him in order to possess her, Abraham told Sarah to say when questioned that she was the man's sister and not his wife. In themselves the words were true, for Sarah was the half sister of Abraham, but it was not the whole truth. Half a lie is always the worst kind of a lie, for, by speaking what by itself, as to the letter, is true, the deceiver creates a false impression. This was a cowardly subterfuge on the part of Abraham, even when we make allowance for the different position of woman in that day, for by this lie Abraham was protected, but his wife was exposed to peril. His sin and fall is an example of how men fall where they are strongest. What was Abraham's strongest trait? His faith in God's guidance and leadership. He could

trust God when he left his own country and took the
long journey into the unknown country. But he
could not trust God when he went down to Egypt.
He could trust God for his destiny and the destiny
of his race, but not for a single incident in his life.
Men often fall on their strongest side. Therefore,
let him that thinketh he standeth take heed lest he
fall. Moses was the meekest man, yet he fell in a
moment of angry presumption when he smote the rock
thrice, and denounced the people as rebels. Elijah
was the prophet of magnificent courage, and yet when
Jezebel sought to kill him, Elijah, under the juniper
tree, asked God to take away his life. Peter was the
apostle of natural and impulsive courage. In the
Garden of Gethsemane, he drew his sword against the
whole mob, and yet the same night he went down before the pointed finger of a serving maid. The
ancient city of Sardis fronted the broad valley of the
Hermos River with the Tmolus Mountain at its back.
The citadel toward the mountain was regarded as so
naturally strong and impregnable that no defense
was made on that side; and there it was that the soldiers of Darius made their ascent and took Sardis.
Abraham, the man of great faith, in this incident of
his life resorts to a miserable and cowardly falsehood. But do not waste any wonder on Abraham.
Be amazed rather at your own heart, its strange in-
consistencies, its oft rebellions, its contrary move-
ments; yes, deceitful above all else is the human heart,

and he that trusts in it is just what the Bible calls him—a fool.

III. The Supreme Test

Reading the biographies of great men, one is struck with the fact that in so many lives there has been one great affection, one great sorrow, and one great trial, the trial usually arising out of the affection or the sorrow. So it was with Abraham. His great affection was Isaac, and his great trial was on Mount Moriah.

The years were going by, and Abraham was now old. His descendants were to be a great nation in whom all humanity was to be blessed. Yet apart from the son of the bondwoman, Ishmael, Abraham had no heir, and almost in despair and wondering how God could fulfil the promise, Abraham one day cried out, "O that Ishmael might live before God!" Then after repeated promises and long postponement Isaac was born. He was dear to Abraham, not merely as the child of his flesh and the son of his old age, but as the channel through whom the promise was to be fulfilled and all nations blessed. Then suddenly, and without warning, came the dreadful blow. Isaac was now a lad of strength and of years. But one evening as he sat beneath the oaks of Mamre the word of God came to Abraham: "Take now thy son, thine only son, Isaac, whom thou lovest, and get thee into the land of Moriah; and offer him there for a burnt offering upon one of the mountains which I will tell thee of."

We have no record of what transpired that night, no intimation of the agonies of Abraham's heart. Isaac! his only beloved son! the child of the promise! and one through whom were to flow blessings to all mankind! And now God tells him to offer him up as a sacrifice! When he pleaded for Sodom and Gomorrah, Abraham stood by the truth, "Shall not the Judge of all the earth do right?" Now he is to be put to the test, to see if he really believes that truth, and how great that test. There is no record of that night of struggle and of tears and of prayers. All we know is that early in the morning Abraham arose and set out with Isaac and the two servants as God bade him.

On the morning of the third day, he could see on the horizon the outlines of the mountains, probably the mountains upon which Jerusalem was builded. There was Moriah, and there he must offer up his son. Driving in and out of so many cemeteries which have the name of Mount Moriah written over them, I fell to wondering why so many cemeteries bear that name. Then I remembered Abraham and Isaac, and the reason was clear. On Mount Moriah Abraham offered up his beloved, and in all these cemeteries men at the command of God and nature offer up their beloved.

Leaving the two servants behind, Abraham put the

wood for the offering on the young shoulders of
Isaac, and with the knife and the fire in his hand
they set out to climb the mountain. Nothing in the
Bible can surpass in pathos the record of that journey up the slopes of Mount Moriah. Isaac said to
Abraham, "Father, you have the fire and I have the
wood for the offering, but where is the lamb? How
can we have a burnt offering without a lamb?" How
that question must have pierced the heart of Abraham
with a knife sharper than that which he held in his
hand. All that Abraham can say, and to be fulfilled
in a way that he could not have seen, was to reply,
"My son, God will provide himself a lamb for a burnt
offering." So they went together, and when they
were come to the place, the summit of the mount,
where afterward the angel appeared unto David, and
stayed the plague, and where the Temple of Solomon
was to be built, Abraham now built the altar, Isaac
assisting him to gather the stones and place the wood
over them, still wondering where the lamb was to
come from. Then, no doubt tenderly, his father disclosed to him the awful truth. He himself was to be
the offering. When he had bound him, Abraham
took the knife to slay him. But even when the blade
was flashing in the sunlight he heard a voice that he
knew so well, "Abraham, lay not thine hand upon the
lad, neither do thou anything unto him, for now I
know that thou fearest God, seeing thou hast not
withheld thy son, thine only son, from me." Lifting

up his eyes, Abraham saw a ram caught by its horns struggling in the thicket. In a moment Isaac was loosed, the ram was substituted, the offering made, and when it was finished Abraham called the place Jehovah-Jireh, "The Lord will provide." The Jews even to this day have a proverb, "In the mountain the Lord will provide," and the meaning is that even in the last extremity God will provide for those who trust him.

> "If called, like Abraham's child, to climb
>   The hill of sacrifice,
> Some angel may be there in time;
>   Deliverance shall arise."

We dismiss all difficulties and profitless discussions as to why or how Abraham could have been asked to do such a thing, and center our thought on the indisputable fact that when God commanded Abraham to offer up his son, his only beloved son, Isaac, he submitted him to the supreme test. Grandly, magnificently, Abraham's faith stood the test. Remember it was not mere blind submission, but the submission of faith, for, as the writer of that grand chapter on faith in his letter to the Hebrews puts it, "By faith Abraham when he was tried, offered up Isaac, accounting that God was able to raise him up even from the dead."

How much can your faith stand? Are we just sunshine soldiers and summer patriots, and will the winter of adversity freeze and wither our confidence and our enthusiasm? Sunshine and prosperity do indeed test us, but not consciously. The point is, what shall we do when God begins to point out Moriah on the horizon of our life? When he takes away wealth, or health, or happiness, or worldly hope, or a child as dear as Isaac was to Abraham? That will be the test. Can we say, "Jehovah-Jireh," "The Lord will provide"? Can we say with that other greatly tested man of the Old Testament, "Though he slay me, yet will I trust him"? "The Lord gave, the Lord hath taken away. Blessed be his name."

God lets us prove him in the same way in which he proved Abraham. When Abraham was about to offer Isaac, God said, "Now I know that thou fearest me, seeing that thou hast not withheld from me thine only son." Now I know! God knows how much faith you have by the way you submit to his tests. Yet God asks us to test him also. He who asked Abraham to offer up his son offered his own Son upon that other mount hard by Mount Moriah, when the earth shook and the graves were opened and the sun was darkened as Christ died for the sins of the world. At Moriah God tried Abraham to see if he believed in God enough to sacrifice his son. On Calvary, God tries you and me, to see if we have faith enough in God to believe that he loves us enough to sacrifice his own Son. Yes, wonderful love, love so amazing, so divine, eternal proof of God's goodness and God's forgiveness, for he that freely offered up his own son

[58]

will not withhold from us any good thing. Now we know! Because Christ died on the Cross, we know that God loves us, and "who shall separate us from the love of Christ? Shall tribulation, or distress, or persecution, or famine, or nakedness, or peril, or sword? Nay, in all these things we are more than conquerors through him that loved us. For I am persuaded that neither death nor life, nor angels nor principalities, nor powers, nor things present, nor things to come, nor height nor depth, nor any other creature shall be able to separate us from the love of God which is in Christ Jesus, our Lord."

V. *Joseph—The most Christ-like man in the Old Testament*

THE world's g r e a t e s t story centers about a lost boy. Pronounce his name, Joseph, and every chord in human nature and human experience commences to vibrate. All the elements of the great story are here—jealousy, love, lust, heartbreak, sorrow, death, affection, and hope.

The story begins on the plains of Dothan, not far from where the plain opens toward Esdraelon and Mount Carmel. To the south are the mountains of Samaria, and to the north and east the mountains of Gilboa. The plain is covered at this season of the year with grass and flowers. The white dots are flocks of sheep; the black dots are the tents of the sons of Jacob, who have come from Hebron, far in the south, to pasture their flocks. One of them looking southward sees the flutter of a garment on the distant horizon. What he saw was the coat of many colors. Seeing it he said to his brethren, "Behold, this dreamer cometh. Come, let us slay him, and we will see what will come of his dreams."

Joseph already had the name of a dreamer. He was the first-born of Rachel, and the half brother to the ten who sold him into captivity. The coat of many colors which his father made for him was the singular badge of Jacob's affection; and also, no doubt, of Jacob's affection for Joseph's dead mother, Rachel. In his dreams Joseph saw the sheaves in the field bow down to this sheaf, and the moon and the sun and the stars doing obeisance to him. This was too much even for Jacob, who rebuked him and said to him, "What is this dream that thou hast dreamed? Shall I and thy mother and thy brethren come to bow down ourselves to thee to the earth!" Yet the thing, no doubt, pleased Jacob, and secretly he treasured Joseph's dream in his heart. Joseph had the first equipment for achievement in life. He was a dreamer, and no great and good thing was ever accomplished where a dream, a vision, a purpose, an ambition, did not first illuminate the way. If there were dreams to sell, what would you buy?

It would, indeed, have been the end of Joseph's dreams, had it not been for the intervention of Reuben, who persuaded his blood-thirsty brothers to put Joseph down in a pit, purposing to release him at a favorable opportunity. But while Reuben was absent with his flocks, the caravan of the Ishmaelites hove in sight, and Judah suggested that they sell him into

Egypt, instead of killing him. The price was twenty pieces of silver, ten less than Christ brought on the market of hatred and envy. Joseph was bound on the back of a camel, the caravan got under way and was soon lost on the southern horizon. The route to Egypt passed near Hebron, and on one of those nights, when the Ishmaelites were resting at their camp, Joseph must have seen in the distance the oaks of Mamre and thought with a pang of his father's tent and how he would never see him again. The next morning the caravan moved southward and Hebron faded out of sight, apparently, forever.

A few nights afterward there was a painful scene at Jacob's tent near Hebron. The cruel brothers brought in Joseph's coat which had been dipped in the blood of one of the goats. Holding it up, one of them said, "This we have found. Can you tell us whether or not it looks like thy son's coat?" Jacob needed no second glance to identify it as the coat of many colors. At once he concluded what his sons desired him to conclude, that a wild beast had devoured his son. The old man, rising from the ground, rent his own garment and put sackcloth on his head. When they saw his great grief, his sons had some compunction of conscience, and with all his daughters rose up to comfort him. But Jacob refused to be comforted, and said, "I will go down into the grave, unto my son, mourning." Jacob had reached the place at which a great many troubled hearts arrive, the place where they feel that there is nothing in store for them but the grave.

The drama of Joseph may be divided into two main acts. Act One: Joseph in Adversity. Act Two: Joseph in Prosperity. We have already witnessed the first scene in Act One—Joseph sold by his brothers into captivity. The next scene opens on a bright morning in a slave market at the capital of the Pharaohs. The captain of the royal guard, Potiphar, comes down to the slave market to look for a likely slave. Passing down the line of captives, who have been brought in from east and west, north and south, Potiphar's eye falls upon Joseph. He examines his body with an expert care, inquires about his nationality, and the bargain is struck. Joseph is to be a slave in the house of Potiphar.

In that situation, instead of moaning over his fate, or exhausting himself in self-pity, Joseph, with an optimism which must have been born of a deep faith in God, resolves to make the best of the situation. If he must be a slave in Egypt, then he will be the best kind of a slave. The result was that the integrity and character and ability of Joseph soon advanced him to the chief post in his master's house. Potiphar saw that his house was blessed for Joseph's sake. That was the finest tribute that could have been paid to Joseph. The house was blessed for his sake. Some houses are blessed or cursed for the sake of those who come to reside in them. But Potiphar felt, as Laban had felt about Joseph's father, Jacob, that the Lord had blessed him for his sake.

Now comes the third scene in this first act. We are to behold Joseph on the arena of temptation. He had come quickly to favor, and, although a slave, to a degree of prosperity. But now the shadow is lurking on the horizon. How will Joseph carry himself in this trial? What he went through, in one form or another, waits for every man, and what will become of a man's dreams depends on what he does on that arena. Looking upon Joseph as he engages in this old, but yet ever new, battle with the tempter, we say to ourselves, Now what will become of his dreams? The best counselors, the best friends, or the fondest parents cannot build a wall high enough to shut out temptation. The best that they can do is to impress upon the mind of youth the fact that they must fight this battle, and that everything which is to come after, influence, character, inward peace and joy, depends upon the issue of the conflict.

From the standpoint of this world it would have been wise for Joseph to yield to the temptation. Not to do so would bring upon him the revenge which did come. Then he was only a slave, and he was far from his father's home. Slaves were not supposed to have morals. Joseph, too, was in the flush and vigor of his youth. He was not a marble statue, nor was he a withered Egyptian mummy. The miracle is that he passed unscathed through the temptation. How was it accomplished?

The sword which Joseph used at that dangerous hour when his whole future depended upon the decision he must render was one which had inscribed upon it, How can I do this great wickedness and sin against God? Joseph had a sword which was made in heaven. What held him back from transgression was not the sense of ingratitude toward his master, although he was conscious of that; nor was it the fear of Potiphar, nor the reflection that he might possibly spoil his career in Egypt; nor was it disgust with and scorn for the temptress. It was the fear of God and the dread to do that which was wicked. Joseph won his battle because he was able to pronounce the most difficult word in any language, Hebrew, Egyptian, English, "No."

Jacob was in many respects a sensual and unworthy man; but there was a mixture of heaven in his clay. He was conscious of divine things and of the divine presence; and although he plunged frequently into sordid sin, he also wrestled all night with the angel, and refused to let him go until he blessed him. From what Joseph did and said in this critical hour, we can be sure that Jacob had not neglected his duty toward this son. He had, indeed, made him a coat of many colors; but he had also given him something of far greater importance, more valuable than any inheritance in money or real estate that a father can leave to his son. He had taught him the fear of God, and that between right and wrong there is an unbridgeable chasm. Joseph knew that the chasm was just as wide and deep in Egypt as it was in Hebron.

When the third scene of Act One opens we see Joseph in the prison. The hatred and revenge of Potiphar's wife has landed him in the dungeon. Joseph has gone to prison for the most honorable act of his career. He was in prison, but in prison with honor. He had been stripped, and yet decorated. In Korea today, if one of the native pastors has not been in a Japanese prison, his congregation have doubts as to his sincerity and his character. Imprisonment, under those circumstances, meant loyalty to Christ and the Gospel. During a trial in one of the courts, a lawyer who was cross-examining a witness from whom he had failed to draw any damaging confession suddenly stopped the line of questioning which he had been following and abruptly asked the man, "Have you ever been in prison?" The man replied, "Once." A gleam of satisfaction came into the face of the attorney who was cross-examining him and was seeking to discredit his testimony. Confident now that he was about to do that, he said to the old man, "When and where were you in prison?" The old man lifted up his shoulders and, drawing his faded blue coat across his breast, for he had been a soldier in the army, answered with almost a shout, "Andersonville!" The courtroom rocked with cheers, and the case was dismissed. Like Joseph, he had been in prison, but with honor.

That first night in the dungeon must have been a hard one for Joseph. He had been true and faithful to the highest, but all that he had won was a dungeon. It would not have been strange if Joseph had now yielded to despair and said to himself, "Virtue, thou art but an empty name. Where is the God of Abraham, Isaac, and Jacob?" But the spirit of Joseph was not broken or soured by his terrible experience. Again his faithfulness and his hopefulness and his kindness serve him well, and he is advanced to the chief post in the prison. The warden hands over all the other prisoners to him to look after. Joseph was the sort of man who comes to the top, no matter where he is placed.

Now come the dreams of his fellow-prisoners, the chief butler and the chief baker, who had offended their lord. The chief baker had dreamed that he had three white baskets on his head, and the birds of the air were eating cakes from the third basket. Joseph, whose sympathy had prompted him to ask the two dreamers why they were so cast down in countenance, interpreted the dream as follows: The three baskets are three days. Within three days Pharaoh shall hang thee on a tree, and the birds shall eat thy flesh. For a man of Joseph's innate tenderness and kindness, it must have been hard to give that interpretation to the unfortunate baker. But the tenderest heart sometimes must speak the severest message. The chief butler had dreamed of a vine with ripe grapes on the branches, and he took the grapes and pressed them into Pharaoh's cup. This, said Joseph, was the interpretation. Yet three days, and Pharaoh shall restore thee unto thy place and thou shalt deliver his cup into his hand. Both interpretations proved to be true. The baker was taken out and hanged; the butler was restored to his post. When he was leaving, Joseph in touching language pleaded with him to show him kindness and speak a word for him to Pharoah. If he did so, he would be assisting an innocent man, for, said Joseph, "I have done nothing that they should put me into the dungeon." Then the prison door banged shut. Joseph went back to his dark dungeon, the chief butler to the sunlight and freedom. One would think that that butler could never have forgotten his benefactor. But the butler was only human. "Yet did not the chief butler remember Joseph, but forgot him." Joseph in the prison was the "forgotten man."

Now we come to Act Two in the drama of Joseph, or Joseph in Prosperity. Pharaoh had a dream. Seven lean ears of corn ate up the seven fat; seven ill-favored cattle ate up the seven fat cattle which fed in a meadow by the bank of the Nile. No one could interpret the dream. Then the ungrateful butler suddenly remembered the Hebrew lad who had interpreted his dream in prison. Joseph was brought out of the dungeon, and quickly told Pharaoh the meaning of his dream. There were to be seven years of plenty, followed by seven years of famine. Some of those who chart the rise and fall of business and money tell us that every seven years there is a decline. No economic system will ever be devised which will banish the lean years from the world, and the timeless lesson of Joseph's political economy is to do what Joseph advised Pharaoh to do in the time of plenty—save for the time of want.

Joseph advised that Pharaoh look out a man discreet and wise and set him over the land of Egypt. The civil works, or famine administrator, selected by Pharaoh was none other than Joseph.

Joseph is now to be tried by prosperity. That is a greater trial than adversity. The man who has fallen heir to a fortune is in greater moral peril than the man who has lost one. Nations in the times of prosperity are in greater danger than in time of adversity. I have heard leaders among the Jews express the fear that the prosperity and plenty of the Hebrew people in the United States might do them more injury than the persecutions to which they have been subjected in other countries. Men and nations can take a lot of hammering; but too much heat enervates them.

How will Joseph take prosperity? Prosperity sometimes makes men forget God. They say, "Is not this great Babylon that I have built?" But Joseph as prime minister of a world empire keeps as close to the God of his fathers as he did when in Potiphar's house, he cried out to the tempter, and to the ages, "How can I do this great wickedness and sin against God?"

Prosperity sometimes makes men hard. They attribute their success solely to their own energy, foresight, and skill; and the ill success of others to indolence, or improvidence. But the more prosperous Joseph became, the more his heart was enlarged.

Prosperity sometimes makes men forget their old friends, their associates of humbler days, and sometimes even their own flesh and blood. But the prime minister of a world empire never forgets the black tents or his father's house. There were days when the tawny palaces along the Nile, with its palm trees and its water wheels, and its colossal pyramids, and the temples of red sandstone with serpents wound about them and silent, staring sphinx in front of them, faded from the view of the prime minister and gave place to Hebron, the black tents, the oaks of Mamre, and the mountains of Judea. "Does my father still live? Or does he sleep now in the cave of Machpelah by the side of Abraham and of Isaac? And my brother, Benjamin—does he still live?" Egypt had made Joseph famous, but his heart was never Egyptianized. He had married the daughter of an Egyptian priest, and his own Hebrew name was changed to an Egyptian name. But when his sons were born he called one Ephraim, "God hath caused me to be fruitful in the land of my affliction"; and the other Manasseh, "God hath made me forget all my toil." The record adds "and all my father's house." But from what follows, it is plain that what Joseph had forgotten was not his father nor his brothers, but the bitterness and the sorrow of his captivity and slavery.

Neither had Jacob forgotten Joseph. Often, we are sure, he thought much about him. I wonder if he ever asked himself, "Did my sons deceive me? Can it be possible that Joseph still lives?" On a day when his sons and their families are afar off with the flocks, Jacob opens an old black chest, and taking from it a faded garment, lays it across his knees. It is the coat of many colors, with the rents and the stain of the blood still there. Tears are in the eyes of the old man, and if any had been at hand, they might have heard him exclaim, "Joseph! Rachel!"

Another famine came, and this sent the brethren of Joseph down into Egypt to buy corn. All the severity which Joseph feigned in his dealings with them, and the tests to which he subjected them, the keeping of Simeon, and the threat to keep Benjamin, and the repeated questions about another brother they had not brought with them, were for the purpose of ascertaining whether or not their hearts were as hard and cruel as ever. But in the midst of the trial, after Judah's eloquent appeal for Benjamin, Joseph

broke down, threw off his stern mask, and said to the
wondering Hebrews, "I am Joseph!"

That was a great scene; but not a greater or more
dramatic than that which took place when Joseph's
brethren returned to Hebron and told Jacob that
Joseph was still alive, and that he was the prime
minister of Egypt. The old man was not able to
take it in. He could not believe it. He thought his
sons were mocking him. But "when he saw the
wagons" he believed, and was carried down into
Egypt and united again to his long-lost son, who fell
on his neck; and, says the chronicler—and no wonder
—"wept a good while." Jacob now was ready to die.
"Now let me die, since I have seen thy face, because
thou art yet alive."

Why do I call Joseph the greatest Christian of
the Old Testament? And why is Joseph thought of
as a type of Christ?

In the first place, Joseph overcame temptation and
kept himself unspotted from the world. He presented his body a living sacrifice unto God. Long
before the Christian apostle taught men that their
body was the temple of the Holy Spirit, Joseph lived
in the light of that truth.

In the second place, Joseph showed a wonderful
forgiveness. When we speak of the Christian spirit,
what do we mean? We do not mean, primarily, the
spirit of resistance to evil, although the Christian
must always do that; nor do we mean the spirit of

prayerfulness, although the Christian must always do that; nor do we mean the spirit of charity and kindness, although the Christian must always be that. What do we mean when we say one has a Christian spirit? We mean that he has a *forgiving* spirit, that he is able to love his enemies, and pray for them that despitefully use him. In the beautiful paraphrase of the author of *Ecce Homo*, "God said, Let there be light, and there was forgiveness."

Joseph was a great Christian, too, in his view of Providence. When his brethren came to him after Jacob's death, and brought to him what was probably a forged message from Jacob, asking that Joseph should forgive his brethren and not take vengeance upon them, Joseph made his great answer, "Fear not, am I in the place of God? As for you, ye thought evil against me, but God meant it unto good." That is the true Christian philosophy of life. At the end Joseph could see how all the trying experiences through which he passed had worked together for his good, and for the good of Egypt, and for the good of his father's house. Long before St. Paul said it, Joseph practiced it—"All things work together for good to them that love God." In the time of trial and trouble, remember that verdict of Joseph—"God meant it unto good."

Joseph was the great Christian, last of all, in his wonderful faith in the future. When he was dying he said to his brethren, "God will surely visit you and bring you out of this land, and ye shall carry up my bones from hence." Joseph was not buried, but put "in a coffin in Egypt" and for four centuries that coffin was to the exiled and now enslaved Hebrews the symbol of faith and hope that God would yet visit his people. And when the hour of deliverance at length struck, they carried the bones of Joseph up with them into the Promised Land.

Egypt, this life, is not all! Canaan, our true home, is yonder! Never forget that promised land! Have faith in it as Joseph had faith that God would visit his people and bring them out of the land of captivity and out of the house of bondage. As Joseph did, keep the heart free of bitterness, unbelief, hatred, envy, and fear. Forget not the true homeland of the soul.

VI. *Samuel—The noblest man in the Old Testament*

ON the eve of his last battle with the Philistines, Saul, haggard and despairing, had asked the witch of Endor to call up Samuel. The woman succeeded better than she expected. This time it was no imposture, but an awful reality, and the woman cried out in fear when a form stood before her. Saul asked her what she saw, for the form was visible only to her. The woman answered, "I see a god coming up out of the earth."

Samuel was godlike even in his death. He is one of the few men of the Bible who can bear such a description. There was a majesty in his life lifting him high above the common ranks of men. In him spiritual and moral powers are predominant. He rises out of the mists of antiquity like a god.

Life is a book of three volumes. A vast number never get past the first volume. A yet larger number go beyond the second volume. Only to a few is it permitted to live through the third and final volume,

and when they do so their life is either a great blessing or a great misfortune. In the life of Samuel,
none of the three volumes is wanting. We begin
with Samuel as a child in his mother's arms, and we
follow him through his long life down to the hour of
his death. Indeed, we commence with Samuel before
he was born, and we hear him speak out of his grave.

Moral greatness requires a preparation and a background, for men do not gather grapes of thorns. To
understand the character of Samuel we must commence before he was born. Back of every great life
lies the mysterious purpose of God. When the world
needs its great man, God has him ready, and there is
a man sent from God whose name is Elijah, or Moses,
or Samuel, or John the Baptist. But in sending
these men into the world, it has often pleased God to
send them through channels and instrumentalities of
which it is possible for us to judge. This is true in
the case of Samuel, for we begin with the prayers of
his godly mother, and her consecration of him to the
service of God's house. When we read the life of
Nero, we are not surprised that his mother was a
murderess; when we read the life of Byron, we are not
surprised that his mother was violent, vain, and pas-
sionate; when we read the life of St. Augustine, we
are not surprised that his mother was a woman of
great prayer; and when we see what John Wesley did,
it is no surprise to learn that he had a great mother

who brought him and her other children constantly before the Throne of Grace.

Samuel, a man of prayer, was himself an answer to prayer. His mother called him Samuel, "I have asked him of the Lord." And when she took him up to the holy house at Shiloh and left him there, it was with this benediction, "I have lent him to the Lord." A classmate of the man at Yale told me this interesting bit of history about a distinguished minister of the Presbyterian Church, now deceased. During their days at Yale, the college was stirred by a revival. Nearly all of the men of their class were moved by this revival except this one student. Years afterward, when he had become a minister, his friend asked him to tell him how it was that, of all the men in their class, he had apparently been untouched by the revival, but was now a useful minister in the Church. The man said that his conscience had not been unstirred by the college revival, but that he had fought against making a confession of his faith, for he feared that if he became a Christian he would then become a minister, and he was determined to make a name for himself as a lawyer.

After graduation he went to a city in Georgia to read law in the office of a prominent attorney of that state, and to act as a tutor to the man's sons. He had been there a year or more when the news came to him that his father had recently died in the Vermont home. His friends had asked him, as he sat by the window and looked out upon the sun sinking behind the western mountains, if he cared to send any word to his son in the South. "Yes," he said, "tell him his mother prayed for him as long as she lived. Tell him his sister Martha prayed for him as long as she lived; and tell him that I died praying for him; and now I leave him in the hands of the Lord." When he read the letter he left his law books and went out into the forest alone. There he fought the battle between his own self-will and the prayers that had been offered for him. The prayers conquered. He determined, not only that he would become a Christian, but that he would become a minister. The gentleman in whose home he had lived, and in whose office he had studied, was greatly disappointed when he announced his intention of forsaking the law. He told him that within a few months he could be admitted to the bar, that he had high ability and was sure to make a mark and a place for himself as a lawyer. Moreover, he desired that he should take his two sons and travel with them in Europe for a year, and then upon his return become his partner.

But his resolution could not be shaken. He packed his belongings, bade his friends farewell, and started for New England, where he entered Andover Seminary. After leaving the Seminary he took charge of a church in a Vermont village. There were children to be baptized, and, not yet being ordained, he asked a neighboring minister and a friend of his father and mother to assist him in the service and administer the sacrament. After the child had been baptized, the visiting minister said to the congregation, "This sacrament of baptism today reminds me of a similar service many years ago. I can see coming down the aisle of the church a tall, handsome man with a babe on his arms, and a lovely young wife at his side. When they came before the pulpit, the mother handed me a card on which was written the child's name and the date of his birth. At the bottom of the card was the word 'over.' I turned the card over and on the reverse side read these words which had been written by the child's mother. 'I hereby dedicate this child to God and to the Gospel ministry.'" "That child," said the minister to the congregation, "is the minister who stands by my side today." Yes, more things are wrought by prayer, and by a mother's prayer, than this world dreams of.

Samuel was put to the test when the Lord spoke to him as he slept in the house at Shiloh. Three times he ran to the old priest, and said, "Here am I, for thou didst call me." The third time, Eli recognized that God, who often hides his secrets from the wise and prudent and reveals them unto babes, was speaking to the child, and told him to answer the next time, "Speak, Lord, for thy servant hearest." Ever after that was the watchword of Samuel's life— to know what the will of God was, and then with all

his heart, soul, strength, and mind to do it. It was
not easy to do what he had to do that night. God
told him that he would make an end of Eli and his
house because of the sins of his sons. In the morning Eli asked him what the Lord had said unto him.
The old priest had a premonition of tidings of judgment, for he charged the child not to hide anything
from him and Samuel told him every whit and hid
nothing from him. That is the kind of minister and
prophet every church should desire to have; not one
who will speak what pleases them, but who will speak
the whole counsel of God and hide nothing that God
hath revealed.

Samuel entered upon the stage of Hebrew history
in a dark and critical hour. The nation was corrupt
and degraded in the very place which ought to have
been the foundation of purity and inspiration, the
tabernacle at Shiloh. Now judgment had fallen, the
Philistines had defeated Israel in battle, Eli and his
sons were dead, and worst of all, the ark of God was
taken. The national situation was summed up in
the name which the expiring daughter of Eli gave
to her new-born child, Ichabod, "The glory is departed from Israel." But it is the darkest just before
the dawn. Man's extremity is God's opportunity.
Again and again in the history of Israel the great men
of the Old Testament appear when the fortunes of
the chosen race are at their lowest ebb. When Ahab
and his wicked Jezebel had filled the land with heathen

idols, and all but exterminated the true religion, then like a thunderbolt, Elijah, the son of the Tishbite, appears on the stage and stands before the wicked king and queen, to pronounce upon them the judgments of the Lord. Again, when infamous Ahaz had filled the land with his abominations, when altars to the stars had been built on the top of the temple, and a chariot to the sun in the temple court, and an altar to Moloch at the city wall, and the lights of the holy house had been put out and the doors of the temple closed, in that dark hour God raised up Hezekiah to do his will and lead the nation back to Jehovah. So in this dark hour, Samuel comes to the front and judges Israel for forty years.

We know very little about that long administration of Samuel, save that it was one of righteousness and justice. Samuel was pre-eminently a man of intercession and prayer, and frequently we hear of his earnest intercessions for the nation. I wonder if any of our public men of today are men of prayer? We hope that some of them are, although we hear nothing of it. When the nation passed through the fiery furnace in the sixties, it had for its leader a man of prayer. When he said toward the end of the war. "Fondly do we hope, fervently do we pray, that this mighty scourge of war shall speedily pass away," there is no doubt that he himself was of the number who most "fervently prayed." We know that he was often on his knees when the thunder of the cannon was rolling toward Washington; and that he not only prayed himself, but invited others to pray with him and for him.

The last chapter in Samuel's life is the saddest and yet the noblest. After his forty years of service to the nation, the leaders of the people came to him and said, "Behold, thou art old, and thy sons walk not in thy ways." Both charges were true. Samuel was old. In the battle with time all of us will lose. Samuel's sons walked not in his ways. That was a mysterious providence for Samuel, for there was no doubt that Samuel had prayed earnestly for his sons, and set before them an example of a godly life. We can understand how David had bad sons who repeated some of his own sins and crimes. But bad sons for Samuel—that is a mystery. Yet now and then God puts some of his noblest saints to that test.

The people wanted a king. They were tired of being ruled by a prophet, which means that they were tired of a reign of righteousness. They wanted to be like the other nations around them which had kings to lead them out into battle. What will Samuel do now? How will he stand in adversity? How will he look when the sun is going down? What shall we see written on his face when adulation and flattery and its fickle crowd are gone, and the man stands alone, wrapped in the mists, with the darkness coming down? Yes, that is the ultimate test. But in that trial Samuel is still godlike.

During the World War there was the story of a Russian soldier who was posted as a sentinel in a dangerous position. The old Russian army had a tradition that when a sentinel had been posted, he could be relieved or withdrawn only by the officer who had posted him, or by the Czar himself. But the officer who had posted this sentinel had been killed in battle, and the soldier refused to leave his post until an order came from the Czar himself. Samuel had been posted as the leader of Israel by God himself, and when he left that post it was not because the people had asked for a king, but because God himself told him to withdraw, for he said, "They have not rejected thee, but me." When Samuel heard that, he yielded to the people's demand and anointed Saul king of Israel. But when he left his public post he took this beautiful and affectionate farewell of his people—"God forbid that I should sin against the Lord in ceasing to pray for you." So Samuel heaped coals of fire upon the heads of the people who had rejected him. He took his revenge by not ceasing to pray for them. Long before Christ stood on the mount and said, "But I say unto you, Love your enemies, do good to them that hate you, and pray for them that despitefully use you," Samuel, godlike prophet, was practicing that code. In a sense, the Gospel was preached before Christ from age to age in the lives of the servants of God who prepared the way for his coming.

The most touching chapter in Samuel's life is his relationship with King Saul. Samuel was taken with Saul the moment he saw him. And who is not taken with Saul? for he had many splendid and lovable traits. With all his faults, he worked his way deep into the hearts of those with whom he came in contact. When he is dead all that David will do is to lament over him, and when the Philistines had mutilated his body and hung it up on the walls of Bethshan, there were still those who loved Saul enough, old soldiers who had followed him in his campaigns, to risk their lives for the sake of his memory, for by night they stormed the town and took his body and the bodies of his sons and cremated them at Jabesh and buried the ashes under a tree.

The tragedy of Saul is the tragedy of the man who knows the right and has moments when he desires to do it, but sets up his own will against the will of God in his life. That is always a tragedy, whether it takes place in our community or in Israel ten centuries before Christ. Samuel saw with grief Saul's departure from obedience. At length, in spite of all his warnings, the time came when Samuel and Saul had to part. "And Samuel came no more to see Saul until the day of his death." That has always struck me as one of the saddest and most solemn verses in the Bible. Samuel came no more to see Saul—Saul whom he had chosen, anointed, loved, and over whom he had prayed. And Samuel himself recognized the sadness of it, for we read that the only time Samuel ever came under the displeasure of God was at this time when his grief for Saul was so intemperate as to interfere with his public duty, and God said to Samuel, "How long wilt thou mourn over Saul?" It is, indeed, a tragic hour when the prophet of God withdraws from the soul of man. Yet God, who loves us and loves us enough to send his only begotten Son to die for us, has made it clear that his Spirit will not ever strive with man. Therefore, resist not the Holy Spirit. Grieve not the Holy Spirit, because when men resist the Holy Spirit and grieve the Holy Spirit, they are preparing the way for the ultimate tragedy, the quenching of the Holy Spirit.

But now the end has come for Saul. The Philistines have again invaded the land, and Saul and his sons go forth in battle to meet them. Pale and haggard, Saul leans on his sword at sunset on Mount Gilboa's slopes. Below in the valley he sees the great army of the Philistines, and the evening wind carries the hum of their host high up the mountain to Saul's camp. Saul was never easily frightened, and he is a soldier to the last. But on the eve of this battle he has misgivings. He reaches out in that hour for a rock that is higher than he. But the oracles were dumb. God answered him not, for the Spirit of the Lord had departed from him. No revelation came to him in a dream. No mystic light flashed from the breastplate of the high priest. No prophet or sons of the prophet could answer him. In his despair Saul knocks on the door of the underworld. What he was going to do now had been outlawed by his own decree. Therefore, Saul goes in disguise to the woman who was reputed to have a familiar spirit; that is, one who could call up the dead. When the haggard king had explained his errand, the crafty impostor asked the usual question, "Whom shall I call up?" What did Saul want? Did he want merely to know what the issue of the morrow's battle would be? Or did he want more than that? Did he want a word of counsel or compassion or encouragement from some of the great servants of God who had lived in the past? There were many whom he might have named—Abraham, Moses, Joshua, Jacob, Gideon. Certainly they could tell him what he wanted to know and fortify the soul. But no! Listen to the word that fell from the lips of the haggard king, as he stands in disguise before the woman in her dark and dismal cave. Not Abraham, Moses, Jacob, Joshua, Gideon; but Samuel! "Bring up Samuel; Samuel who anointed me as king. I mocked at his counsel; I disobeyed his injunctions. But now the night is dark. Priest nor prophet, dream nor mystic stone will answer me. Call up the man who once kissed me before my lips were defiled with falsehood and my heart with rebellion. Call up the man who loved me and yet ever told me the truth. If I am to perish in tomorrow's battle, he will tell me. Call up the man who went down to his grave mourning for me. If any man can help me or instruct me now, it is he. Call up Samuel!"

Beautiful, tender, magnificent tribute! Alas, that Saul had not realized in his life what Samuel could do for him, and sought his counsel only when he was dead. That is often true of human relationships and friendships. Yet what a tribute this is to Samuel, that he is the one King Saul would bring out of the other world. Saul, some think, was a regenerate man, because we are told that God gave him another heart and that he was turned into another man. But if a regenerate man, his life is an illustration of how a man can waste his gifts and be a tragic failure, saved, and yet saved only, as Paul said, by fire. I would not say that this final request of Saul for the presence of Samuel was a sign of grace and repentance in Saul's heart; although it looks like it. The one with whom we are dealing now is not Saul, but Samuel. Call up Samuel! He lived so near to God and spoke God's truth so clearly, fearlessly, earnestly, that when he was dead men longed for his presence, and even the King of Israel asked for his presence. Call up Samuel! That is the way we ought to try to live, so that when all three volumes of life are written, and the story is closed, there shall be those who in some hour of perplexity, or trial, or sorrow, will think of us and say and pray, as Saul did for his dead friend, "Call up Samuel!"

VII. *Elijah—The loneliest and grandest man in the Old Testament*

ELIJAH comes upon the stage of Israel's history like a crash of thunder. He disappears from it in a whirlwind. From the beginning of his history to the end of it, he is a man of thunder and lightning, of fire and whirlwind. Whenever he appears, the lightning flashes, the thunder crashes, the fire flames, and there is a sound of a mighty wind.

Yet, when Jesus Christ was on earth men thought that he was like Elijah, so much so that some said he was Elijah come back to earth again. The Old Testament came to a close with a prophecy by Malachi, that God would send Elijah the prophet before the great and terrible day of the Lord came; and that he would turn the hearts of the fathers to the children, and the hearts of the children to their fathers. It was not strange, then, that men were looking for Elijah, although the prophecy was fulfilled in the ministry of John the Baptist. It is a mistake to make Christ all benevolence and goodness, and to forget that he was also the minister of righteousness and of judgment. Men who listened to him were reminded of the thunder and lightning of Elijah. Elijah, then, in a way, was Christlike. This we say, not only on the testimony of this popular verdict, but on the ground of the honor bestowed upon Elijah when Christ was transfigured. Elijah was one of the two men from Old Testament times who were distinguished with the honor of talking with our Lord concerning his coming death on the Cross. If Christ, then, found it worth while to talk with Elijah on the Mount about the work of redemption, certainly it will be of profit to you and me to spend a few moments in conversation with this great prophet.

Why do I call him the loneliest and grandest man of the Old Testament? He was the loneliest because, unlike some of the great servants of God in the Old Testament and in the New Testament, Elijah had no reliance upon, or help from, wife, family, friends, or associates. Always, save at the very end of his career, Elijah appears alone. He was alone in his stand against the iniquity of his day, and as Isaiah said of the passion of Christ, so Elijah could say, "I have trod the wine press alone, and of the people there was none to help." He was the grandest man of the Old Testament because of his solitary and heroic stand for righteousness against a wicked king and queen, the organized religion of the day, and practically the whole population of the kingdom. Elijah appears and disappears by himself. Lonely, and yet how grand!

By the authority of Jesus Christ himself, we can measure Elijah and his greatness by John the Baptist. John the Baptist, Christ declared, was as great a man as ever lived. When his disciples asked Jesus about the prophecy that Elijah was to come again, Jesus answered that he had already come; and the disciples understood that what Jesus meant was that Elijah had come to earth again in the spirit and ministry of John the Baptist.

Elijah and John have a remarkable similarity. They wore the same kind of clothes. Elijah was a hairy man and girt with a girdle of leather about his loins; while John was clothed with camel's hair and with a girdle of a skin about his loins. Elijah and John were both schooled in the desert. They were the sons of solitude. Both of them graduated *magna cum laude* at the University of the Desert, with the degree of M.S., Master of Solitude. Both prophets had to proclaim messages of judgment and denunciation. Both displayed superb courage— Elijah denouncing Ahab and Jezebel; and John the Baptist, Herod and Herodias. Both were pursued by the hatred and enmity of a wicked woman—Elijah by Jezebel, and John by Herodias. Both prophets suffered a temporary eclipse of their faith—Elijah, when he asked God beneath the juniper tree to take away his life; and John in the prison of Herod, when he sent his message to Jesus, "Art thou he that should come, or look we for another?" Both are immortal in their influence. Elijah! John the Baptist! Either name is like an army with banners. Elijah's greatest recognition and reward was to stand on the Mount of Transfiguration and talk with Christ about his crucifixion; John had the almost equal recognition of preparing the way for the ministry of Christ. Each may be described as the loneliest and grandest man of his age and dispensation.

Israel was in a bad way. As far as we can tell, in a more desperate situation than at any time in her long history. Jeroboam had given the nation a push toward idolatry when he set up his golden calves at the two extremities of the kingdom, Dan and Bethel. But there was no open and public renunciation of the worship of Jehovah. But now, when Ahab is on the throne and is married to a daughter of an idolatrous king, all pretense is thrown aside and the worship of Jehovah is proscribed. A great temple for the brutal and licentious and degrading worship of Baal, the bull-god, was set up at Samaria; and another great temple for the worship of the unclean Ashtaroth at Jezreel. The prophets of Jehovah and the priests were hunted over the hills of Samaria like wild animals, and in the whole population of Israel there were only seven thousand who had not gone over to the worship of Baal. It looked as if Ahab and Jezebel had accomplished their purpose, and that the true religion had been destroyed.

But as has often been the case in the history of Israel and of the Church, the darkest hour was followed by the dawn. As Christ at the fourth watch of the night came walking over the stormy sea to the frightened disciples, so again and again God has come with deliverance just when it seemed that all was lost. Suddenly God acts! Without warning, without introduction, Elijah the Tishbite stands before the apostate king of Israel and pronounces judgment upon his kingdom. "As the Lord God of Israel liveth, before whom I stand, there shall not be dew nor rain these years, but according to my word."

That dramatic appearance of Elijah was the beginning of a process of national reform and recovery. Whichever way they turn now, this guilty king and queen, there stands the grand and fearless prophet to defy them with his "Thus saith the Lord." This emergence of Elijah and his heroic ministry is of a nature to encourage God's people in any dark and troublous hour. It lets us know that, although wrong may seem to be firmly seated on the throne, and truth ever led to the scaffold, behind the shadow God is keeping watch over his own. He says to the raging and swelling sea of human rebellion and sin, "Hitherto shalt thou come, but no further; and here shalt thy proud waves be stayed."

The history of Elijah is a powerful demonstration

of the influence of a single personality. God is never through with great men. The world today affords a striking illustration of the power of individuals and the sway they can exert over masses of mankind. We see this in the dictator of Turkey, Kemal; in Stalin of Russia; in Hitler of Germany; in Mussolini of Italy. Whether their policies are good or bad, and whether they themselves are good or evil men, the power which they exert over millions of their fellow-men is a striking witness to what a single life can accomplish. In the history of redemption, God works through great men, who are the "inspired texts of the book of Revelation, a chapter of which is completed from epoch to epoch, and by some called history."

Elijah, who played this grand part on the stage of Israel's history, was not an initiator, nor a discoverer, nor a founder like Moses. What he did was to declare and reaffirm the great principles of righteousness. The truths which he spoke were those which had been well known but abandoned by the people. What our country and what our Church needs today is a ministry and witness like that of Elijah. We do not need more laws—we have too many already. What we need is respect to the laws we have. We do not need more knowledge or science, but more will power. We do not need more theology, especially "new" theology, but faith in what we have. The nation's chief need is not new schemes of industry and finance and politics, but a return to the God who established it and made it great.

Elijah's grand victory over the priests of Baal on Mount Carmel, when at his prayer the fire from heaven fell and consumed his offering, is perhaps the climax of his ministry. Nothing in the history of Israel compares with that stupendous scene—the futile howling of the priests of Baal; the intercession of Elijah when the sun was going down; the fire from heaven; the killing of the false prophets; and then the sound of the coming of the rain. But it was only a short journey for Elijah from this mountain top of exultation and victory to the valley of depression and despair. He seems to have expected that, after this public overthrow of the false worship, the king and the queen would turn from their idolatry. But he reckoned not with the strong-minded and ferocious Jezebel. Fleeing from her persecuting hand, Elijah fell at length fainting and exhausted beneath the juniper tree in the desert, and said to God, "It is no use. I am no better than my fathers. They were not able to root out iniquity in their day; neither can I. It is enough. O Lord, take away my life!" This was no childish pique or petty disappointment. Like John the Baptist in prison, Elijah was troubled about the cause of righteousness in the world. It seemed to be going down. He did not care to live to see its fall. He had given all the energies of his soul to what seemed to be a lost cause. All was in vain.

God might as well let him die. At least, if the work was to go on, others would have to carry it.

I have always found a degree of comfort in reflecting upon Elijah under the juniper tree, and John the Baptist in the prison of Herod. If mighty souls like these could suffer an eclipse, then it need not trouble us that there are times when you and I are depressed and almost in despair concerning that same great cause of truth and righteousness in the world. There are many today who are perplexed, confused, and some disheartened because of the iniquity which has come in upon us like a flood. What, we are tempted to say, has been accomplished by all the witness and struggle of the past on the part of Christ's true Church to the Kingdom of God? Neither men nor nations seem to be willing to learn by experience. But in the darkest hours we must remember that God has not abdicated his throne. When the great Negro orator, Frederick Douglas, was speaking at an antislavery meeting in a hall at Salem, Ohio, in the Forties, in the bitterness of his soul he seemed to sound a note of pessimism and almost despair for the future of the black race. Then a voice was heard crying from the gallery, "Frederick, Frederick, is God dead?" It was the voice of the famous Negress and advocate of freedom, Sojourner Truth. Elijah learned that God was not dead, and much as he himself wanted at that time to die, he discovers soon that it is the wicked Ahab and

the wicked Jezebel who are to die, and not God's
prophet, Elijah.

> "Oh, it is hard to work for God,
>   To rise and take His part
> Upon this battle-field of earth,
>   And sometimes not lose heart!
>
> He hides Himself so wondrously,
>   As though there were no God:
> He is least seen when all the powers
>   Of ill are most abroad.
>
> Or He deserts us at the hour
>   The fight is all but lost;
> And seems to leave us to ourselves
>   Just when we need Him most.
>
> Workman of God! O, lose not heart,
>   But learn what God is like;
> And in the darkest battle-field
>   Thou shalt know where to strike.
>
> Thrice blest is he to whom is given
>   The instinct that can tell
> That God is on the field when He
>   Is most invisible." [1]

Everything about Elijah is grand, and yet nothing grander than his end. Nothing became him in
his life like the leaving of it. We see him go forth
toward the Jordan with the faithful Elisha, although
Elijah tenderly sought to persuade him to remain

[1] Bishop Frederick W. Faber.

behind. His robe opens a path through the Jordan, and when Elisha has made his prayer for a double portion of his great master's spirit, chariots and horses of fire appear, and Elijah is carried up to heaven in a whirlwind. Gazing after him, Elisha exclaimed, "My father, my father, the chariot of Israel and the horsemen thereof." A true and splendid summary of Elijah! As the horses and chariots led the van in ancient battle, opening the way for the infantry to follow, so Elijah with his devotion to truth and his immense faith and courage was the horsemen and the chariots of his people.

Was it all worth while? When it was over, this grand and lonely life, was it worth while? Did Elijah ever think that it might have been better to have acquiesced in the iniquity of his day, muffled his great voice, become a chaplain to Ahab and Jezebel with comfortable quarters in their ivory palace? He might have done that, but he chose God, loneliness, suffering, and immortality. Not in the same way, but much the same as to principle, we today are called upon to make the choice. Is the faithful, sacrificial, self-denying, Christian life worth while? Are not the pleasures of life and of the world, after all, to be preferred? Many conclude that they are. But the wise will remember that the satisfactions of the world are only for a season, that Christ and faith are forever and ever.

Elijah cried out to the assembled nation of his day,

"How long halt ye between two opinions? If the Lord be God, follow him; but if Baal, follow him." The same choice goes on from generation to generation. If some have decided for God, and today are wavering, may the example of Elijah call you back to your faith. If some are still halting between two opinions, may the voice of Elijah call you to choose Christ and Eternal Life.

Elijah cast a long shadow after him. Generations after he was dead, men looked earnestly into the faces of the great ones of the earth to see if Elijah had come back to life. On the Mount of Transfiguration, Moses and Elijah appeared with him in glory and spake with him concerning his death at Jerusalem. Moses and Elijah! Moses, certainly; we can understand that, for he wrote of Christ, and through him came the Law. But why Moses and *Elijah?* Why not Moses and Isaiah, the great prophet who described so touchingly the death of Christ? Why not Moses and Abraham, through whom the first covenant was made? Why not Moses and David, who sang of Christ, his sufferings, his glory, and his never-ending Kingdom? But the record of the Gospels is not Moses and Isaiah, nor Moses and Abraham, nor Moses and David, but Moses and Elijah. In an age of wickedness and apostasy Elijah stood alone for God, faced the confederated powers of iniquity, offered himself for the salvation of his people. Now Christ on his way to the Cross, looking forward to the last great battle on Calvary, finds inspiration and comfort in talking with the mighty Elijah. We wonder what he said to Elijah, and what Elijah said to him. Imagination cannot compass it! But when he came down from the Mount, Christ marches straight toward the battlefield of the Cross. On the Cross he hung between two thieves. Perhaps, who knows, there were others there, too, one on either side: Moses who wrote of him, and Elijah to whom it was granted not to die because he had been so true to God.

VIII. *Jacob—The worst and the best man in the Old Testament*

JACOB is the best and worst man of the Old Testament. That interests you and me, for we all know a worst within us, and we all hope that there is also a better and a best. Jacob is one of the least difficult characters of the Old Testament for us to study and estimate, partly because we know so much about him—what he did the moment he was born, his youth, his manhood, his old age, and even his dreams—and partly because he is a man of like passions with us. Abraham, Moses, Samuel, and Elijah are almost too great and too grand for us, although one of them, Elijah, was called by James "a man of like passions with us." They excite our admiration and our reverence and veneration; but we cannot feel that we are as close to them as we are to Jacob, in whom the good and the bad follow each other in quick succession. When you think of Jacob, there are two things which will come at once to your mind, two scenes from his life—first, Jacob cheating

Esau out of the blessing and deceiving his blind and aged father; and second, a ladder of gold, the top of which reached to heaven, with the angels ascending and descending. There is Jacob, the worst and most despicable man in the Old Testament in that first scene; but, in the second scene, the man who can talk with heaven.

In Jacob you behold the everlasting struggle between good and evil for the mastery of a man's soul. What strange contrasts there are in Jacob—cheater, liar, deceiver, and yet the man who can dream of heaven and wrestle with an angel. Pascal in his celebrated *Thoughts* thus describes the heart of man: "What a chimera, then, is man! what a novelty, what a monster, what a chaos, what a subject of contradiction, what a prodigy! A judge of all things, feeble worm of the earth, depositary of the truth, cloaca of uncertainty and error, the glory and the shame of the universe!"

That was man, the heart of universal man, man in the image of God, and yet fallen and sinful, that Pascal described; and there, too, is Jacob, the glory and the shame of the Old Testament. You may call his life the drama of the winning of the soul. God chose him at the beginning—"Jacob I have loved." Although Jacob struggled hard against the hand and the purpose of God, in the end he comes at length to strength and beauty of character. He had power over the angel and prevailed. And there is our life—

temptation, sin, trial, discipline, sorrow, suffering, Gethsemane agony, star-lit hopes, golden ladders of aspiration and prayer, tumultuous passion, measureless affection and love, midnight struggles, and the peace and beauty of the evening.

I. JACOB'S SIN

It was a divided family which lived at Beersheba, for Isaac loved Esau, but Rebekah loved Jacob. Perhaps the reason for that was that Rebekah pondered in her heart the strange words which had been spoken at the birth of her son, how the elder should serve the younger. One day Esau, the man of the open air, and a hunter, while his brother stayed about the encampment, came in from the fields hot and hungry, and, smelling the pottage which Jacob was cooking, asked him for a portion of it.

Nothing could have been more crafty and despicable than the way in which Jacob took advantage of the fierce hunger of his brother, bargaining with him to let him eat of the pottage if Esau would give him the birthright. Esau is to be despised, and in the New Testament is handed down to posterity as "that profane" man because he despised his birthright. That is true; yet, afterward, he sought earnestly to get it back. He despised his birthright in a moment of physical appetite and desire, but when he came to himself he realized the terrible blunder he had made and sought, though unavailingly, to correct it. But

he had committed the irrevocable. The birthright
had been sold to Jacob for a mess of pottage. Esau
found no place for repentance, though he sought it
carefully and with tears. Alas, how much a man can
give away in a moment of time! All our sympathies,
however, are with Esau in this incident. Jacob has
our contempt. Yet there is a golden strand running
through the fabric of his infamy, for it was the birthright, something more than flocks and herds, that
Jacob aspired to possess. Probably he would not
have cheated or lied to secure the goods of Esau.

The next scene presents Jacob in an even worse
light than the last. The only redeeming feature is
that the deceit and villainy which he practiced on his
father and on his brother were suggested and en-
gineered by his mother. Rebekah was animated, it is
true, by great ambitions for her son. Yet it was she
who suggested to Jacob the mean and despicable deceit which he practiced on this occasion. What
character in the Old Testament excites our contempt
and disgust to the degree that Jacob does when we
see him coming in to the presence of his blind and
aged father with the meat of the kids he has killed
and prepared in the vessel and skins upon his hands
and arms, so that when Isaac feels him he will be
convinced that it is Jacob, and not Esau? There is
Jacob at his worst. Strange foundation, you say, on
which to build the glorious structure of a chosen people and a world's redemption. Yet so, it pleased

God. "Jacob I have loved." I once said in a sermon on Jacob that, looking at the two men, Jacob and Esau, I wondered that the Lord had chosen and loved Jacob rather than Esau. A Jew who chanced to be present wrote me the next day, taking exception to what I had said, and remarked that I knew better than God. There was something timely in his criticism; yet on the surface appearance of the two men, Esau probably would get the popular vote.

Once again Jacob has cheated and supplanted Esau. But as soon as his father is dead Esau plans his vengeance. He determines in his heart to kill Jacob. And who would blame him? Rebekah gets wind of the plot and sends Jacob to far-off Haran in Mesopotamia to visit the people of her brother Laban. "Tarry with him," she said, "a few days until thy brother's anger turn away from thee and he forget that which thou hast done to him. Then I will send and fetch thee from thence." Rebekah in her fond, loving heart thought that the separation would be only for a little period. But when she kissed Jacob goodbye that day, it was, so far as this world was concerned, forever. Jacob never saw her face again.

If there is one lesson which the life of Jacob teaches above all others, it is that a man's sins will find him out. It doesn't matter in which direction he travels, or how far he travels. Be sure your sins will find you out. The record here is that Jacob went out from Beersheba. It was the threatening vengeance of his brother that made him flee. But the real cause was the sin of Jacob which had brought down upon him his brother's wrath. Sin always drives a man out, away from his home, away from his friends, away from his joy, and away from his peace. Our first parents sinned and went out from the Garden of Eden, where the angel with the flaming sword kept the way of the tree of life. Gehazi sinned and lied to the prophet, and went out from Elisha, a leper white as snow. Peter denied his Lord and went out from his presence. Cain slew his brother and went out from the presence of the Lord. Judas let Satan enter into his heart and went out from the Last Supper and from the presence of Christ—"and it was night." That is what sin always does—always out, always away from the presence of the Lord.

Jacob's dream at Bethel is one of the loveliest things in the Bible. How swift and complete the change from the lying, deceiving wretch with the venison in his hands and the skins on his arms to the youth who sleeps at the foot of the ladder whose top reaches to heaven. Poets, painters, hymn writers, preachers, all have paused at Bethel and tried to describe that scene. The fact, however, is that no words can add anything to the simple beauty of the Old Testament narrative. To say much about it is like attempting to paint the lily or refine the gold. Suffice it to say that just at the time when he needed him most, when he was lonely, frightened, homesick, smitten in conscience, Jacob discovers that God is near, that God is merciful and forgiving, and, upon the condition of his faith and obedience, will bless him and care for him wherever he goes.

Probably all of us have had, or shall have, some one experience in life when God seemed nearer to us, real beyond any question or doubt, than he was at any other time. It may have been the moment of joy and happiness, fulfilled desire, or that moment of disappointment and despair, the time of temptation, the hour of sin; but whenever the time or place or hour, you can always say of it, "This was the gate of heaven, this was the house of God."

When the morning came, Jacob took the stone upon which his head had rested, set it up for a pillar, poured oil upon it as a sign of consecration and worship, and, kneeling down before it, vowed that if God was with him wherever he went, and brought him again to his father's home in safety and peace, he would come there to Bethel and worship.

Probably thirty years passed before Jacob kept that vow. Down in Mesopotamia, getting along in the world, outwitting his unscrupulous uncle, Laban, increasing in flocks and herds, Jacob seems to us very far removed from the Jacob who vowed at Bethel; just as far as cattle troughs are from the angels at the gate of heaven. But when he finally obeyed the voice of God, buried the idols that his family had accumulated, and returned to Bethel and worshiped there, God blessed him again.

What about your vows? Did you never make a vow in some hour of peril and danger, of awakening conscience, or in the moment of spiritual uplift and aspiration, or when your heart was softened with sorrow, or stirred with the goodness of God? Have you kept that vow? Somewhere, and you know best where it is, there is a stone which once you set up as Jacob did at Bethel. When you go back to it and keep your vow, God will bless you again. And how many times you and I need to be blessed and refreshed in this long pilgrimage of life!

II. JACOB IN HARAN

All the world loves a lover. In this respect, no fault can be found with Jacob. All the affection of his strong and rich nature flowed out to the lithesome maid, Rachel, whom he first saw when she came to water her flocks that morning at the well outside the town of Laban. Forever after, one woman holds all his love. This was love at first sight. In the case of his father and mother, Isaac and Rebekah, the order was marriage, and then courtship, and love. But here it was the more natural order—love, courtship, marriage. Laban made Jacob serve him seven years for the hand of Rachel, and they seemed to Jacob as so many days, for the love he had to her. That is one of the finest things said of Jacob; and, as Coleridge has remarked, "No man who could love like that could be wholly bad." Love lights the path of life, not only this kind of love, but all other kinds. Hate makes the day seem long, and its hours to drag, and the soul wonders when the day will end. Love makes the days seem short. Its hours pass like a flash, and the heart dreads when the day will come to an end.

III. The Midnight Battle

Jacob is now on his way back to his own country. He has made good in the world. He has wives, children, flocks, and herds; whereas, when he landed in that country, he had nothing but his staff. Now he returns a rich and powerful, almost a famous man. But there is a shadow across his path, and in that shadow Jacob sees a face—Esau. A guilty conscience unnerves one in the hour of danger. When Jacob hears that Esau is coming to meet him, and four hundred armed men with him, he is afraid.

But twenty years have passed since his crime against Esau. Was it not possible that in these two decades of time Esau had forgotten all about that offense of Jacob, or, if he did remember it, it was without bitterness and only with pity for the brother who deceived him? Rebekah had said that Jacob was to stay in Haran until Esau's wrath was turned away and he had forgotten all about the wrong done him by Jacob. That was quite possible; and, as the event turned out, all the bitterness is gone from Esau's heart. He is great and magnanimous in his forgiveness, as Jacob had been mean and despicable in his crime against him. When the two men finally met, Esau, instead of killing Jacob, ran to meet him and fell on his neck and kissed him. A beautiful scene! Esau loved his enemy and prayed for him that had despitefully used him.

But, although Esau could forget and forgive the sin of Jacob, Jacob cannot forget it. This night his sin is terribly alive. Twenty years have passed. Esau married; Jacob married; changes in their lives and fortunes. But now the infamy and sin of Jacob come back to him with all the freshness of twenty years ago. How strange, and yet how terrible, is the vitality of sin! You may have changed, life may have changed, but your sin comes back unchanged.

> "What is this power
> That recollects the distant past,
> And makes this hour,
> Unlike the last,
> Pregnant with life,
> Calling across the deep
> To things that slumber, men that sleep?
> They rise by number
> And with stealthy tread,
> Like a battalion's tread,
> Marshal our dead.
>
> This is the gift
> Men cannot bargain with nor shift;
> Which went with Dives
> Down to Hell,

With Lazarus up to Heaven;
Which will not let us e'er forget
The sins of years,
Though washed with tears.
Whate'er it be,
Men call it Memory." [1]

In his distress Jacob calls upon God. What he says is this, "O God of my father Abraham, and God of my father Isaac, I am not worthy of the least of all the mercies and of all the truth which thou hast shown to thy servant." There are times when a man feels just that way, wholly unworthy of God's goodness and mercy, unworthy to call upon God in prayer at all, and when he does pray he approaches the mercy seat pleading the faithfulness and goodness of God unto a godly father and mother. That is a great inheritance; and when you feel unworthy to pray yourself, or to ask anything on your own behalf, you can ask it on behalf of a godly father or a praying mother. "O God of my father, and God of my mother, deliver me and help me."

With his usual resourcefulness, Jacob did all he could to protect himself and his family from the supposed vengeance of Esau. In the night he passed his family and his possessions, his flocks and herds, over the brook; but, held by some unaccountable instinct, he himself remained alone on the other side. Here when we come to tell what happened, let us remove our shoes from off our feet, for the ground upon

[1] Author unknown.

which we stand is holy. "And Jacob was left alone, and there wrestled a man with him until the breaking of the day."

Sublime, mysterious, unapproachable conflict! Others in the Old Testament speak with God, plead with him; but here is a man who struggles and wrestles with God. What is of concern to you and me in that strange midnight encounter is the result of it. Jacob struggling desperately with the angel said, "I will not let thee go except thou bless me!" The angel did bless him. His name up to this time, and his life up to this time, was Jacob, the supplanter, the deceiver. But now the angel gives him a new name, Israel—henceforth, forever, the name of God's chosen people, the name of his Church, the name of his redeemed. Israel means power with God. Henceforth Jacob is a new man. He is a regenerated man. Christ said that must happen to us all. "Ye must be born again." But when confronted with that mystery, remember that you *can* be born again, and determine that you *will* be born again.

Others have struggled at the midnight hour, struggling with they hardly knew not, man or angel, god or demon; a struggle as hard and long and lonely as that of Jacob. Thousands of souls are at their Jabbok now. Hold on to God, as Jacob did to this angel. Say to the angel of your experience, however hard or dark it may seem now, "I will not let thee go except thou bless me."

Now comes the last act in this long and stormy drama of Jacob's life. Jacob is regenerated, forgiven, transformed, a prince with God; but still his sin finds him out. As he had done, so the Lord requited him. It is a long journey from the camp at Beersheba, where Jacob deceived his father and cheated his brother, to the camp at Hebron, where the brothers of Joseph hold up a coat all torn and stained with blood, and ask the father if it is the coat of Joseph. Jacob had one great sin in his life, one great love and affection, Rachel; and now one great and supreme sorrow. Joseph is dead, at least the cruel brothers deceive him into that conviction. There is nothing left for Jacob now but to go down into the grave with Joseph mourning.

Driving through South Carolina, I stopped at Georgetown, perhaps the oldest settlement in the state. In the harbor was a ship, a four-masted schooner. On a ship something like that one bright spring day in 1813, Theodosia Burr, the wife of the governor of South Carolina, set sail from Georgetown to visit her father, Aaron Burr, at New York. Aaron Burr was a bad man, although brilliant. The one good thing in his life was his consuming affection for this beautiful daughter, Theodosia. The ship on which Theodosia sailed from Georgetown never reached port, never was heard of again. Long years afterward, one might have seen an old man leaning on his staff, standing on the waterfront at the Battery at New York, looking off seaward through dimming eyes to see if the ship which bore his daughter was coming into the harbor. But the ship never came.

In the life of Jacob, the sad story of separation had a different ending. The ship comes back with his lost son on board. Joseph still lives, and Jacob goes down to Egypt to meet him again. Now his heart is satisfied. Life holds nothing further for him and he is ready to go. When he struggled with the angel by the Jabbok, he wanted to know the name of his adversary, the name of God. Now, as he blesses when he dies the sons of Joseph and lays his hands upon their heads, it is not the mystery, the unexplainable in God about which he is thinking, but God's great love and goodness, for what he says is this, "The God who fed me all my life long unto this day, the angel which redeemed me from all evil, bless the lads." That is a real triumph of faith, when at the end of the long journey one can say, as Jacob did, "The best I can leave you and ask for you is the God who has fed me and led me and blessed me." At the end, Jacob discovered that the name of God is love. Nothing better was ever said of Jacob than Charles Wesley said in his great hymn:

> "Come, O thou traveller unknown,
> Whom still I hold but cannot see!
> My company before is gone,
> And I am left alone with Thee;

With Thee all night I mean to stay,
And wrestle till the break of day.

Yield to me now, for I am weak,
  But confident in self-despair;
Speak to my heart, in blessings speak;
  Be conquered by my instant prayer.
Speak or Thou never hence shalt move,
And tell me if Thy Name be Love.

My prayer hath power with God; the grace
  Unspeakable I now receive;
Through faith I see Thee face to face—
  I see Thee face to face and live!
In vain I have not wept and strove—
Thy nature and Thy Name is Love."

IX. *Saul—The greatest shipwreck in the Old Testament*

THAT was the end of Saul. It was not the end that might have been, or the end that the prophet Samuel had predicted for him when he anointed him as king and told him that for him was "all that was desirable in Israel." Yet it was the end which Saul chose for himself. Only Saul could destroy himself. That is true of us all. Our best friend and our best enemy is ourself. What circumstances, time, others do to you is of little importance compared with what you do to yourself. "Thou art the man!"

There is no braver sight than a sailing vessel under a full set of sails driving through the sea. It is the incarnation of power and grace and beauty. But there is no more dismal and melancholy sight than a shipwreck—sails gone, mast gone, rudder gone, crew gone; and the waves sounding a melancholy requiem as they break over the decks of the lost ship. Saul is a shipwreck, and, when we take into consideration his great opportunity, his many splendid traits and gifts, the greatest shipwreck of the Bible.

The history of the soul is always interesting, and when we come to deal with the tragedy of soul, the accidents of time and place are thrown aside and we feel our unity with the men of all ages. That is one reason why the story of Saul is one of the most gripping in the Old Testament. It pictures a man of like passions with you and me struggling with circumstance and fate in his life. The personality of Saul exerts a strange fascination, even down to our time. That fascination was felt by all with whom he came in contact; the women of Israel whom he clothed in scarlet; the soldiers in his army who followed him in battle; the prophet Samuel who chose him as king and wept over his fall; Jonathan, his son, who stood by him to the last and fell at his side on Mount Gilboa; and David, whom he sought so often to kill, and yet who loved him, and who, when he heard that Saul was dead, remembered only his noble side and said of him and Jonathan, "They were lovely and pleasant in their lives, and in their death they were not divided."

I. Saul's Morning

Nothing could have been brighter and fairer. It is so with all lives. There is a bright and unclouded morning before the heavens are clouded with sorrow, before the pilgrim falls over the stones of stumbling and the sad music of sin and transgression is heard. In that bright morning Saul set out to seek his father's lost asses. What a day that was! A youth goes out to hunt for lost asses and finds a kingdom. He is thrust out onto the difficult arena of life, where he is to meet his particular trial and test and go down before it.

There is always the incalculable in life. One can never tell what a day may bring forth. Saul goes out in the morning to hunt for asses and comes back at evening a crowned king. The massive gates of circumstance turn upon the slightest hinges of chance. Ruth went out to glean in the fields, and it was her hap, her chance, to light upon that part of the field belonging to Boaz. That chance brought her the bread of life and made her the mother of a great destiny, the ancestress, on the human side, of our Lord. Ahasuerus found himself unable to sleep one night, and called for his secretaries to read to him from the records of his kingdom. Out of that sleepless night of the king came the discovery of the plot against the Jews and the salvation of that people. Columbus, disheartened and discouraged, on his way home from the court of Spain, stopped at the gate of a Franciscan convent near Palos and asked for bread and water for his child. The prior of the convent called together a company of mariners and had them listen to the great projects of Columbus. This was followed by another, and successful, appeal to the court of Spain. Within two years, the frail caravels of the great mariner lay rocking at anchor off the palm-fringed shores of San Salvador. A chance stop at a convent door led to the discovery of a continent.

What we can see taking place on the elevated stage of world history is ever going on in human life today. We go out tomorrow as we have gone on every other; but on this day we shall meet perhaps one of those turning points, one of those tenth hours, in life and destiny. The threads of life, to a surface view, seem loose and entangled. But life begins to show how these threads are working together in the loom of destiny, and that "there is a divinity that shapes our ends, rough hew them how we will."

Looking upon Saul when he first saw him, Samuel said, "For thee is all that is desirable in Israel." So, in a sense, God's prophet says to use all. Life throws open to us great and notable doors. Saul is not the only man for whom is all that is desirable. We all have our unclouded morning, when the prophet meets us, as it were, and points the path to a happy destiny. Unfortunately, like Saul, not all follow the path that has been pointed out.

Samuel told Saul that on his way back to his father's house, on the hill of God, he would meet a band of prophets, and that when the Spirit of the Lord came upon him he would be "turned into another man." This very thing happened. On the hill of God, Saul was given a new heart and turned him into another man. We all have that possibility. A man can degrade himself, brutalize himself, refuse the invitation and the warnings of God's Holy Spirit, and turn himself into another man, that is, a worse man, and thus uncrown himself. Life for us all has that terrible possibility and power. But only God can turn us into a better man. We can turn ourselves into a worse man; but only God into a better man. This is something that happens only by the power of God. Yet God can make use of means in effecting this change: a sermon, a hymn's haunting refrain, a morning wind, someone's death, a word of counsel or warning, the swift awakening of conscience. By ways such as these God can turn us into *another man*. Is that your greatest need today? And ought your prayer to be, "Lord, turn me into another man"?

Nothing could have been more promising than the start Saul made as king. He commenced with that major chord of all great lives sounding in him, humility. After Samuel has crowned him king, he goes back to his father's house and says nothing of it; and finally he has to be dragged out from his hiding place among the baggage of the camp and presented to the people in all the magnificence of his physical frame and stature.

But, as is always the case, great courage lay side by side with deep humility. John the Baptist was a humble man, saying that he was not worthy to untie the sandal strings of the One to whom he was bearing witness; and yet side by side with that humility was splendid, incorruptible, indomitable courage, such as the world has rarely seen. It was so with Saul. The man who was unwilling to be made king, now, when he hears that kinsmen of his people are besieged at Jabesh-Gilead and like to perish at the hand of the Ammonites, displays courage and energy, and rallying the whole nation to arms with his stirring call, marches to the relief of the besieged inhabitants. When Saul was dead and his body desecrated and nailed to a Philistine wall, we shall see how the men of Jabesh-Gilead remembered his deliverance.

But more remarkable even than his humility and his courage on this first field of battle was Saul's magnanimity. When he came back from his victory over the Ammonites, his enthusiastic supporters wanted to take vengeance upon those who had despised Saul when he was crowned king, the children of Belial, who said, "Shall this man reign over us?" But Saul, never more a king than at that moment, refused to satisfy himself with a petty vengeance, but said, "There shall not a man be put to death this day, for today the Lord hath wrought salvation in Israel." Never was Saul so mentally and morally tall, so head and shoulder over all Israel, as when he forgave the enemies who had despised him.

II. Saul's Breakdown and Failure

Thus far all has been fair and prosperous, not a

cloud on the horizon. But as in a summer sky the clouds quickly gather, quickly now the sky of Saul's life is dark and overcast. Saul had not asked to be king. Conceivably, he might have lived a quiet and peaceful and happy life, had he not been thrust out upon that great arena. This was the place where he was to be tried. All of us must meet our test, and it never comes of our own choosing.

Now we begin to see the other Saul, that other and worse man, who waits his opportunity within us all. The first failure was at Gilgal. The Philistines had invaded the country, and Samuel had told Saul to wait seven days before he engaged the battle, until he came to the army. But the seven days passed, and Samuel came not. Saul's heart was filled with misgiving as he surveyed the thirty thousand chariots and six thousand horsemen, and foot soldiers as the sand on the seashore in the Philistine camp; and fearing that his army would disintegrate, he himself offered the burnt offering. The smoke of the offering was still ascending when Samuel put in his appearance and said to Saul, "What hast thou done?" To our view the offense of Saul seems almost excusable. But God's ways are not our ways, and he submits us to the severest tests, and asks for obedience and reliance unto the smallest detail of duty. Saul had a ready excuse. He said that he feared the Philistines would join the battle before he had made the offerings and asked for the help of the Lord. "I forced myself,

therefore," he said, "and offered a burnt offering."
Certainly Saul there is a man of like passions with
you and me, for how often we say to ourselves, "I
forced myself. I did not want to do it; it troubled
my conscience to do it; nevertheless, under the circumstances, there was nothing else to do."

Saul's next offense shows a rapid progress in evil,
for now his act is one of open disobedience and de-
fiance, and when called to account for it, he defends
himself with hypocrisy and falsehood. He had spared
of the people of Amalek, the king, Agag, and the best
of the spoils. This he did, not, as he falsely said to
Samuel, to sacrifice unto the Lord, but to make a
display before the people; and it was not, as he said
again, the people of his army who had done it, but
Saul himself. When Samuel heard of the disobedience
of Saul and this second offense, he cried unto the
Lord all night. Happy is the man who has a friend
like that, one who will remember him with his tears
and his prayers before the throne of the Lord. There
are plenty of sunshine friends and fair weather ad-
mirers and flatterers; but the friend who counts is
one like Samuel who will mourn over us before the
Lord.

Samuel, all through this great drama, plays, in a
sense, the part of God. When Saul sins Samuel appears on the scene, as conscience ever comes to meet
us when we have done wrong, to point out the sin and
call us back to obedience. When he was rebuked by

Samuel, Saul said, "I have sinned." If you read through the story of Saul, you will discover this fact, that no one in the Bible uttered those words as frequently as Saul. Whenever he is brought up by the hand of the Lord, and the error of his ways is pointed out, Saul exclaims, "I have sinned!"

Was he insincere in this confession? I do not think that he was. Who can doubt the sincerity of it, for instance, when touched by the magnanimity of David, who had spared his life when he was asleep, Saul cried out with tears, "I have sinned; I have played the fool, and have erred exceedingly"? No; Saul was not insincere. Give him credit, at least, for that. The trouble with Saul was that he did not act upon his repentance, and after each one of these confessions of sin we turn the page and find him walking the same path again. But why throw stones at Saul? Have we not all done that? Felt the folly of our ways, confessed that we had done wrong, and then gone back to it again? We all need to pray, when in a penitential and confessing mood, that God shall reap what he has sown in our hearts, and that the feelings and emotions of a moment of contrition and repentance shall not be lost and wasted.

III. Sunset and Night

At length, we come to the record, "and Samuel came no more to see Saul until the day of his death." That means that Samuel has given up Saul; and

Samuel, remember, takes the part of God in this drama. Sad, unutterably sad, are those words, and only the Bible has the courage to pronounce them, "Samuel came no more to see Saul until the day of his death." Separated from Samuel, Saul now drifts rapidly toward his doom. What a drama it is! Strong passions, fearful flames of jealousy, murder, and hatred; and yet, in the midst of it all, tears of remorse and contrition, words of deep affection for David; and at the end, a pathetic appeal for the help and intervention of Samuel.

Samuel had told Saul that God would take the kingdom from him and give it to a neighbor of his, "a man that is better than thou." Let that phrase be ever in your mind when you read the subsequent history of Saul. Above all characters in history, Saul displays the devastating and corrupting and blasting and withering power of jealousy in a great and splendid life. More than any other character in history, perhaps, Saul illustrates the thesis of Othello, that "jealousy is the green-eyed monster that doth mock the meat it feeds upon." And a wiser than Shakespeare said, "Love is strong as death; and jealousy as cruel as the grave; the coals thereof are coals of fire which hath a most vehement flame." If we need a definition of the evil spirit which came upon Saul and ruled him henceforth, let it be this— jealousy. In the beginning the spirit of the Lord had turned Saul into another man. Now hatred and jealousy turn him into still another and a worse man. We see him swept with the waves of anger and passion and jealousy, ready to kill anyone, ready to suspicion all—David, Jonathan, his own household, and his own devoted soldiers. How dreadful is the human heart without God! Yet in the midst of the storm there come brief moments of sanity, gleams of sunlight, when you feel that even yet Saul will come to himself and be saved. When he was seeking the death of David at Naioth, and messenger after messenger had returned without accomplishing that end, in his rage Saul himself set out to go to Naioth and kill David with his own hand. But on the way he met a band of prophets and once again, as at the beginning of his stormy life, Saul becomes a prophet and prophesies with the prophets. I take this to mean that God, who allows no man to go to destruction without warnings, without appeals, and except over divine obstacles, was making a last appeal to the soul of Saul. But the appeal was in vain.

The next we hear of Saul, it is not God's appeal to Saul through Samuel, or through special grace and providence, but Saul's vain appeal to God. He inquired of the Lord, and the Lord answered him not. Only the Bible has the courage to say a thing like that. God has withdrawn from the soul of Saul. Saul himself must have been convinced of that, for before his last battle he resorted to the witch of Endor.

Pale and haggard, leaning on his sword on Mount Gilboa, Saul surveyed the host of the Philistines as they lay all along the valley beneath him. When a man is right within himself, he has the expectation of the morning and the light; but when a man is wrong within his soul, as Saul was, he has the premonition of the coming night. The woman with the familiar spirit, when Saul came in disguise to her den, asked of the king, "Whom shall I call up?" What was the answer? Who could help Saul in that dark hour? Moses, perhaps; or Abraham; or Jacob; or Joshua; or Gideon. But for none of these did the doomed king ask. What he said was, "Call up Samuel! Samuel, the prophet of God, who anointed me and kissed me when I was made king in the bright morning of my life, ere my heart departed from the Lord; Samuel, who cried all night unto the Lord when I broke the commandment of God; Samuel, who warned me and pleaded with me, but all in vain, and at length departed from me. Call up Samuel!" Something beautiful, touching, and sublime, beyond all words to describe, was that prayer of Saul for Samuel. But he had turned to Samuel too late; and all that Samuel could do was to pronounce his doom and to say, "Tomorrow shalt thou and thy sons be with me."

So Saul comes to his end. In the battle the next day he took a sword and fell upon it. An appropriate ending for Saul's life. God called him, Samuel instructed him; and yet, in spite of all, he perished by his own hand. The great lesson of his life for you and me is this, "Seek ye the Lord while he may be found, and call upon him when he is near." Saul turned to seek the Lord when he could not be found. God makes that plain, unspeakably solemn truth though it is, that his Spirit which calls us to him and which gives us all our day and opportunity, will not always strive with man. There came the day when Samuel came no more to see Saul until the day of his death. The same thing is possible for you and me. If you determine to do it, you can quench the Holy Spirit. But the Holy Spirit, speaking to your heart, is never quenched until it has first been grieved and resisted. God never departs from a soul until that soul departs from him. Therefore, "Seek ye the Lord while he may be found." You can find him now. "Call upon him when he is near." He is near to you now. Now!

X. *Lot—The man who loved the world so well that he lost it*

THERE are some men in the Bible who impress you, not as wholly bad, for no one is that, but as men whose whole life lies on the side of evil. Then there are others whose whole life lies on the side of good. The distinction which is made by the sacred chronicler between the kings of Israel, when he says of some that they did that which was right in the sight of the Lord, and of others that they did that which was evil, is a verdict which can be fairly passed on most of the characters who appear on the stage of Bible history. But there are a few who impress you as not altogether given over to the dominion of evil, nor yet loyal to the right. They are strange combinations of good and evil, like Balaam, who desired to die the death of the righteous, but so lived that he met the fate of the wicked. To this class belongs Lot, who had enough righteousness in him to abhor the iniquities and infamies of Sodom, and yet loved the world so much that he took up his residence in Sodom and almost shared in its doom. Peter refers to Lot as "just Lot," and calls him "a righteous man." But this, at first, seems at variance with the record of Lot in the Old Testament, where he appears, almost always, in an unenviable light. He was righteous, however, in contrast with the foul licentiousness of Sodom. A man of great advantages and great opportunities, Lot must be put down as one of those men who, if saved at all, are saved as by fire. He lost everything he had, his property and his reputation, and passes from history in a dark scene of which it would be a shame even to speak. The secret of his failure and disaster was his love for this present world.

When Abraham went out not knowing whither he went, he took his nephew, Lot, with him. The phrase, "and Lot went with him," is frequently repeated. That means that he had daring enough to go out with Abraham, share in his journeys, his perils, and, at length, in his prosperity. Wherever Abraham goes, Lot goes with him.

The flocks of Abraham and the flocks of Lot had so multiplied that there was not room for both of them in the same part of the country. The land was not able to bear them. Strife arose between the herdsmen of Abraham and those of Lot. The course taken by Abraham was both magnanimous and wise. He refused to be a party to strife with Lot, and although it was his right to choose, and Lot owed everything to him, Abraham said to his nephew, "Let there be no strife, I pray thee, between me and thee, for we be brethren. Is not the whole land before thee? Separate thyself, I pray thee, from me. If thou wilt take the left hand, then I will go to the right; or if thou depart to the right hand, then I will go to the left."

Abraham settled the dispute on the ground of friendship and kinship. There must be no strife, he said, because "we be brethren." Ultimately, that is true of the whole family of nations, for God, as Paul eloquently said on Mars' Hill, "hath made of one blood all nations of men for to dwell on all the face of the earth." We sometimes refer to the Civil War as the "Brothers' War," and such, indeed, it was, for often brother was found fighting against brother. But in the larger sense, every war is a brothers' war, and wars will not cease until men come to recognize and own their brotherhood in the family of God. What an example Abraham is here, not only to nations, but to families and to individuals. The way to settle a quarrel is to refuse to fight, to recognize that whatever is gained by fighting, the gain is out of all proportion to the loss. Abraham in this respect saw Christ afar off, for in the dispute with Lot he did exactly what Christ recommended. Nor did he suffer from the course which he followed; for as soon as Lot has made his choice, God tells Abraham that all the land which he can see will be his, and that of his descendants, forever. "Arise, walk through the land in the length of it and in the breadth of it, for I will give it unto thee." Even from the viewpoint of earthly interests, men do not suffer when they take a generous and Christian course.

Standing on the high rocks of Bethel, Lot surveyed the rich country of the plain of Jordan, well watered like the garden of the Lord, and as fertile as the land of Egypt. Even to this day, coming down toward Jericho from Jerusalem, one can see a belt of green and pleasant oases in the plain of the Jordan. But then the whole valley was cultivated. Lot quickly decided that this was the place for him to settle. He said goodbye to Abraham and set his cattle and his people on the march for the valley of the Jordan.

Lot certainly had acted wisely from the standpoint of this world, for the rich valley of the Jordan was a much better country than the stony hills of the uplands; and yet, in another sense, his choice was not wise. That is brought out in the brief comment of the sacred writer. "Lot dwelt in the cities of the plain, and pitched his tent toward Sodom. *But* the men of Sodom were wicked and sinners before the Lord exceedingly."

Lot must have known that. But it made no difference to him. He was interested only in profits, in crops, in the increase of his goods and his flocks and herds. The fact that he had to live in proximity to sinners and degenerates made no difference to him.

His choice, therefore, was without any regard for principle. He prefers material well-being to moral safety and health. In this respect Lot is quite modern, for, although in a different way, the same choice is presented to men today, and not a few choose exactly as Lot did. If a city in the United States were demonstrated to be the most wicked city on earth, and residence there fatal to belief and morality, and yet a place which conferred material prosperity on every inhabitant, every train leaving Pittsburgh for that city would be crowded with prospective settlers. But that was not the way America was settled. New England was not really a settlement; it was a conviction. Material prosperity was not the motive that brought the Pilgrims through the stormy seas to the bleak coasts and rugged hills of New England. The difference between North America and South America, between the strength and the prosperity of the United States and the backwardness of the Latin republics of South America, is not to be explained on the ground of resources or age of settlement, for South America has the advantage on both points, but to the fact that those who settled South America were looking for gold and worldly prosperity, whereas those who settled New England came in search of God and in loyalty to the truth.

Lot pitched his tent toward Sodom. That would indicate that he did not actually take up his abode in the city, but settled in its vicinity. If anyone at that time had told Lot that in six months, or in a year, he would be an inhabitant of Sodom, a member of its town counsel, and the father-in-law of Sodomites, Lot would have been shocked and would have said it was unthinkable; and yet that is just what happened. When we next hear of him he is living in Sodom, a prosperous and influential citizen there, and his family have intermarried with the Sodomites. All this was natural, perhaps inevitable, because Lot pitched his tent toward Sodom.

Along the highway of life, there is what we might call a twilight region between light and darkness, a border territory between right and wrong. There is a way which leads to sin, and upon which it is always dangerous to venture. There are some acts which cannot be described as positively sinful, but which certainly tend in that direction. There is a way which, although not yet involved in darkness, lies in the twilight between day and night. The way to avoid Sodom and its fate is to pitch your tent in another direction. The drift of a man's life, or the set of his sails, you might call it, is a good indication of the place to which he is going. Mr. Bryan used to tell of a man in his town in Illinois who had been the victim of drink. He reformed, signed the pledge, and apparently was delivered out of his evil habit. But when he rode into town he continued to hitch his horse to the rail in front of the tavern. He pitched his tent toward Sodom, and soon was again a drunkard. The way to avoid evil is to avoid the appearance of it.

Perhaps Lot's wife had something to do with his going into Sodom. It may be that she told him that there was no society for their daughters out there on the plain in the black tents of the Bedoin, and that if their family was to amount to anything they must move into the city and live a fashionable life. If so, Lot was not the first man who came into a city with religious training and background and heredity and possessed of religious principles and then abandoned them. Sometimes they prospered, and very often they suffered disgrace and humiliation, either through their own conduct or the conduct of their children, and lost in the end, as Lot did, even their earthly possessions. Life in the city without principle, without Christian faith, is a dangerous thing, and is likely to end, as in the case of Lot, in moral, spiritual, and material bankruptcy.

Lot had one warning which ought to have brought him to himself. The kings of the east made a raid through the Jordan Valley, sacked Sodom, carried off much booty and a number of prisoners, among whom was Lot. As soon as Abraham heard that Lot had been captured, he showed that he could fight as well as pray and build altars; and setting out in pursuit with his three hundred trained servants, he came upon the booty-laden kings at night, smote them, and rescued Lot and his goods and his family from slavery. This ought to have warned Lot. God does not let men go to destruction without frequent warnings. There are providences which shake a man out of his ease and indifference and sinful comfort; and yet as soon as the peril is passed he sinks back into his old ways. So it was with Lot. He ought to have gone with Abraham, but he went back to his old life in Sodom.

Now comes the drama of destruction. God comes to visit Abraham at the oaks of Mamre and tells him that Sodom and Gomorrah are to be destroyed. God destroys no city and no people until it is rotten to the core. That was the condition of Sodom. The very name of the city has been given to the most odious of human vices. What does Abraham do when he hears of the impending doom? Did he say, "That's just what they deserve. The world will be a better place if those wicked cities of the plain are blotted from off the map. They would have it so. Let them reap what they have sown"? But no; instead of that, Abraham poured out to God his beautiful and noble intercession for the doomed cities. Taking his stand upon the truth that the God of all the earth will do right, and therefore will not destroy the righteous with the wicked, Abraham asks God if he will not spare the place if fifty righteous are found in it. The fact that he begins his intercession with a number so low as fifty shows the terrible condition of these cities. Then he gets the promise that

God will spare the place if forty-five good men are found in it. Then forty, and then thirty, and then twenty, and finally, ten. If ten righteous men are found there, God will not destroy it. When we see what goes on in the world, sometimes we may wonder why God doesn't destroy it, wipe it out with a flood, and start all over again. The reason may be that here and there, scattered over the earth, in every town, in every city, there are still righteous men who fear God and keep his commandments. A good man is the greatest asset of any city.

Those who deserve to be saved are to have their warning. The angels of warning and of destruction appear at Sodom at the eventide and find Lot sitting in the gate, a post of honor and distinction. Lot is at his best when he rises up to greet them, for he seems to be conscious of their superior nature and authority. They propose to pass the night in the streets of the city, but Lot insists that they come under his roof. They accept his invitation and turn in for the night. But as soon as the word of their presence has spread through the city, a mob of Sodomites gather and demand that the men be brought forth. When a man faces a mob unafraid, you can take your hat off to him. It is the highest example of moral courage. Lot faced this howling mob, and said that he would defend them to the last. No one who had come under his roof should suffer harm. The bond of hospitality is sacred. They had come,

he said, under the shadow of his home. We admire
Lot for his courage, even if, making all due allowance
for a difference in standards, we despise him for the
proposal that he made to these degenerates concerning his own family. That very night the angels in-
formed Lot that the cities would be destroyed, and
told him to go out and warn any other members of his
family that they might escape its fate. Lot hurried
out and went to his sons-in-law to warn them saying,
"Up, get you out of this place, for the Lord will
destroy this city." And what happened? "He
seemed as one that mocked unto his sons-in-law."
They laughed and said, "Who is this who has suddenly turned preacher?" They looked up at the
Syrian sky, cloudless and serene, and heard the hum
of the traders about them on the streets, and said,
"Where are the signs of destruction? The old man is
trying to work a practical joke on us. Who is the
Lord anyway, and who cares what he will do?"

That must have been a sad and bitter hour for Lot.
Never was he more earnest and sincere in his life when
he warned his sons-in-law and their families to flee
from Sodom. But they took him as a joke. He had
said so little about the Lord, had seemed to care so
little about him, that now when he speaks for the
Lord, he seems like a man who is mocking, making
use of sacred names and solemn truths for the purposes of a joke. Sad is that record: "He seemed to
them as one who mocked."

In the seminary there was a man in the class above me who was converted and brought into the ministry by an unusual experience. After leaving college he became the secretary to one of the United States Senators from a nearby state. A party had gone with this Senator on a campaign through his state. There was plenty of whiskey and champagne and all that goes with it. In all this the young secretary was a willing participant. One night they were in their room in the hotel, and their life that evening had been in keeping with what had been going on before. Preparing for bed, this young man was surprised to see one of his fellow-secretaries kneeling in the attitude of prayer at the side of the bed. They had heard him mock and had seen him drunk, but never before had they seen him pray. They thought that he was just mocking, putting up a joke on them. One of them gave the kneeling man a push with his foot, whereupon the unresisting body fell limply to the floor, with wide-open eyes staring up at the ceiling. The man was dead. The incident shocked this other young man into sobriety, and turned his steps toward the church. If you got down to pray, are there those who would conclude at first that you were mocking? If you should speak to anyone in the name of the Lord, or warn anyone from the consequences of sin, would you seem to him, as Lot to his sons-in-law, as one that mocked?

Now the time had come to flee the city. But still

Lot lingered. What made him linger? I suppose he could not just bring himself, at the very end, to the thought of giving up all the wealth and possessions that he had amassed by compromise with conscience during his long residence in Sodom. Would it really go up in smoke and come down in ashes? Everything to be wiped out! Lot lingered. So men linger, even when the evidence is plain and the voices of angels are speaking in their ears.

But if Lot lingered, the angels did not, for they took Lot and his wife by the hand, laid hold upon them, and led them out of the city, saying to them, "Escape for thy life. Look not behind thee, neither stay thou in all the plain, but escape to the mountain, lest thou be consumed." Even then Lot still is reluctant to go, and makes a weak and whining prayer that he be permitted to go to a nearby village of Zoar, instead of to the far-off mountain. It was a weak, miserable prayer, which showed that Lot, while willing at the very last to leave Sodom, wants to remain as near to it as possible. Still, even with the smell of brimstone in the air, Lot is the man who would pitch his tent toward Sodom. Yet God grants his prayer, and lets him escape to Zoar, and for his sake spares that city.

Most of the judgments and catastrophes recorded in the Bible are those which happened by night. But this was a more fearful judgment. It was a judgment of the day. It was a sunrise and not a sunset judgment. "The sun was risen upon the earth, when the Lord rained upon Sodom brimstone and fire, and overthrew those cities and all the plain and all the inhabitants of the city and all that which grew upon the ground." The destruction of Sodom is a monument to the fact that God hates sin, and that he will punish it. The Gospel is based upon the fact that sin is a dark and terrible thing, so terrible, indeed, and so deserving of God's wrath and curse, that nothing less than the awful tragedy of Calvary can save a man from sin.

Today the sight of Sodom and Gomorrah is one of the most melancholy, dismal, and depressing places on the face of the earth. Dreary stretches of sand, with tufts of coarse grass scattered over it, and the monotonous oily waste of the Dead Sea. This is Sodom. Gloom, judgment, retribution are written everywhere upon the face of the plain where once stood the prosperous and wicked cities.

Christ preached one of his most telling sermons on the destruction of Sodom, and the one whom he singles out is not Lot, but Lot's wife. "Remember Lot's wife." Lot's wife perished because she *looked* back. She looked back because she *longed* back. Her heart was still in Sodom. Christ was speaking about future judgments, and especially those in connection with his Second Advent. There would be the same wickedness in the world, the same skepticism and unbelief that there was in the days of Lot. Whoever would be saved in that day must give himself wholly to Christ. "Remember Lot's wife." She turned back and perished. "Whosoever shall seek to save his life shall lose it." That was true of Lot's wife. In a sense, that was true of Lot himself. He tried to make the best out of two worlds. He had exchanged his principles and his convictions for worldly prosperity. Now he beholds everything swept away in the flaming judgment which fell upon Sodom, and in a few days he himself passes from the scene in a loathsome cave of drunken incest. "Remember Lot's wife" was Christ's text; but he might have added also, "Remember Lot." The fate of Lot makes you think of the question God propounded to the rich fool in Christ's parable, "Whose, then, shall those things be?"

If the destruction of Sodom makes us tremble at the righteousness of God, God's mercy to Lot makes us wonder at his love. When Lot lingered the angels took him by the hand. The angels still take men by the hand, men who will not be reasoned with and will not be warned. Does conscience reproach you for some past sin, or for some present evil habit? Has your heart been touched by a sorrow or an affliction? Are there times when you have a deep, if fleeting, desire to be a better person than you are now? Do you sometimes think of a child or a parent who is in heaven and wish that you were fit to go there too? Are there times when your heart is moved by the story of Christ's death for sinners on the Cross? If so, these are God's angels. They come to take you by the hand. Perhaps they are taking someone by the hand today. Whether the angels will come back tomorrow or next Sunday, you know not. But if you feel their touch upon your hand, if you hear them say, as they said to Lot, "Escape for thy life," then turn not away from the angel. Do what he tells you to do. Go in the direction he points.

"A greater than Jonas is here."

MATTHEW 12: 41.

XI. *Jonah — The greatest preacher in the Old Testament*

THAT was Jonah's supreme distinction. He was compared with Christ as a preacher, and that by Christ himself. Among all the prophets, patriarchs, and sibyls whose features appear in the ceiling of the Sistine Chapel, the most beautiful and most notable, beyond all question, is that of Jonah. His figure is one in which strength and grace, beauty and mystery, are mingled. Michelangelo felt the spell which Jonah has cast over the minds of every age. When you go down into the Catacombs and see the tracings of early Christian art on the walls of those chambers, the most familiar figure is Jonah, and the great fish as a symbol of the Resurrection. Jonah is the best known character of the Bible, although the popular knowledge of him has to do merely with the incident of the great fish, and not with his preaching and his character.

"The word of the Lord came unto Jonah." We read that frequently in the Old Testament, and

[143]

ask ourselves, How did it come? How did these men know that it was the word of God that had come to them, and not some word of man, or of their own imagination? Sometimes the coming of the word of the Lord was accompanied by signs and wonders, as when God spake to Moses at the burning bush. But whether in some visible and miraculous manner or otherwise, when God sent his word it came with the true certificate of its divine origin. The problem was not to know whether God had spoken, but whether those to whom he had spoken would do his will. God still sends his word, only today he speaks to us through the written word and through his Church. His word may come, too, in some special moving of the Spirit, or conviction of the soul. There is no one today who has not felt at some time a divine compulsion.

This time the word of the Lord said to Jonah, "Arise, go to Nineveh that great city and cry against it, for their wickedness is come up before me." For six hundred years Nineveh was the mistress of the world, perhaps the greatest empire of antiquity. Mounds of human heads marked the triumphal march of her warrior kings across the world, and their sculptured monuments tell the grim story of conquest and extermination. Yet the Hebrew prophets predicted the overthrow and annihilation of the cruel city. The prophets Nahum and Zephaniah describe the siege of the city and its complete desolation.

Zephaniah says that "herds shall lie down in the midst of her; both the pelican and the porcupine shall lodge in the chapiters thereof." Because the city is vile, her grave is dug. These predictions were literally fulfilled. Other empires were subjugated; Nineveh was annihilated. Two hundred years after the fall of Nineveh, Xenophon, marching with the ten thousand Greeks, passed near the site of Nineveh and noted the heap of ruins. But not a man in the army knew what city it had been. It was not until the year 1865, when almost two thousand five hundred years had passed, that the spade of the archaeologist brought to light the ruins of Nineveh. But in the days of Jonah the city was at the height of its splendor, power, and wickedness. God is not indifferent to the condition of cities, nations, and individuals. Behind the shadow he keeps watch over the world. Now, in far-off Galilee, the prophet Jonah receives the commission to go to Nineveh and cry against it.

This was something new in the prophetic office. Hitherto, the prophets had pronounced judgment upon the heathen nations, but at a long distance, within the confines of their own kingdom. But now Jonah is told to go in person to Nineveh and cry against it, calling upon it to repent or to perish. Jonah did not relish his commission. In the first place, it meant a long, difficult, and dangerous journey; and, in the second place, he could not under-

stand why God wanted Nineveh to repent, or why he
didn't destroy it without sending a preacher. Jonah
shared in the patriotic hatred of what the prophet
Nahum called "the bloody city, full of lies and rob-
bery." Instead, therefore, of obeying the command
and starting for Nineveh, Jonah rose up to flee from
the presence of the Lord. Why did he not stay
where he was? If he was determined not to go to
Nineveh, why not stay where he was? Because that
voice was sounding in his ears, "Arise, go to Nineveh." That voice disobeyed made him unhappy and
uneasy. That is true not only of Jonah, but of you
and me. When the voice says, "Go," when conscience
says, "Let it be done," we are uneasy and unhappy
when we refuse, and we try to forget the voice and
get away from the presence of the Lord in the business or pleasure of the world. Evil always makes a
man want to turn away from the presence of the
Lord, even as the first murderer went out from the
presence of the Lord. Why do some men never go
to church, or read the Bible, or kneel in prayer?
Because to do so produces unhappy emotions. Their
first thought is to keep as far away as possible from
anything that will remind them of the voice of God
speaking to the soul.

Jonah made his way toward the seacoast and came
down to Joppa, until a few years ago the one sea-
port of Palestine. Centuries later, in that same Joppa,
Peter on the flat roof of one of the white houses,

sleeping before dinner, had his dream of the great sheet let down from heaven, filled with things clean and unclean; and soon after the interpretation of his dream in the person of the Roman centurion, Cornelius, to whom Peter preached the Gospel. To this same Joppa, where Peter had his vision of the universal Gospel, a Gospel not for Jews only, but for men of every race, Jonah comes fleeing from the command to preach the Gospel to Nineveh.

We can see him walking along the water front and inquiring of the shipping men where this or that vessel is sailing. "Whither bound is this ship, mariner?" "Bound for Tyre with the evening wind." But that is much too near the Lord's country for Jonah. "Whither is this ship bound?" he asks another mariner. "Bound for Egypt." "Too near!" murmurs Jonah, and moves on. "Where is this ship bound?" "Bound for Greece." "Too near!" says Jonah, and goes on down the water front until he comes to the last ship. He says to one of its sailors, "Whither bound?" "Bound for Tarshish." "That's the place for me!" says Jonah. Just where Tarshish was we cannot be sure today, but we know that it was one of the remotest ports known to navigators. That was the place for Jonah. "I'll go to Tarshish," he says, "and there I will hear no more the voice of the Lord." So he paid the fare thereof and went aboard the vessel. At length, when the evening breeze springs up, the anchors are weighed, the sails are hoisted on the horizontal masts, the ship gets under way, and the gray-brown hills of Palestine begin to fade away until they are only a blur on the eastern horizon. With a sigh of relief, Jonah goes below, and finding a dry corner, wraps his prophet's mantle about him and is soon fast asleep, oblivious to the shouts of the crew, the creaking of the ship's gear, and the beating of the waves against her timbers.

But Jonah had not reckoned on one thing. God also goes to sea. God is not through with Jonah yet. "Whither shall I go from thy Spirit, or whither shall I flee from thy presence? If I ascend up into heaven thou art there; if I make my bed in hell, behold, thou art there." Jonah is soon to discover the truth of what the psalmist said. Jonah had boarded a ship bound for Tarshish. But God is not through with him. *"But the Lord sent out a great wind into the sea, and there was a mighty tempest in the sea, so that the ship was likely to be broken."* This must have been the sort of storm described in the 107th Psalm. "He commandeth and raiseth the stormy wind which lifteth up the waves thereof. They mount up to the heaven, they go down again to the depths. Their soul is melted because of their trouble. They reel to and fro and stagger like a drunken man, and are at their wit's end."

The mariners of this ship were at their wit's end as the little vessel tossed like a cork in the midst of the waves. It is said that an atheist is never found among seamen. Wicked men are found among them, but not atheists; for they that go down to the sea in ships, these see the works of the Lord and his wonders in the deep. These mariners, although idolaters, were not atheists. They cried every man unto his god, the god of whatever country he came from, whether it was the god of Egypt, or of Greece, or of Tarshish. But still the tempest raged. Then they lightened the ship by casting its cargo into the sea. But still their situation was desperate, and the ship rolled at the mercy of the wind and the wave.

Through all this tumult Jonah, down in the sides of the ship, was sound asleep. The Bible speaks of a drunken man who will sleep on top of a mast. Jonah was not drunk with strong wine, but he was drunk with the poison of his sin and rebellion. The fact that he can sleep so soundly, and never hear the rolling of the casks, the slapping of the sails, the smashing of the spars and gear, the shouts of the mariners, the howl of the gale, and the crashing of the waves, shows how far gone Jonah was. Fleeing from the face of the Lord, he can sleep in the midst of the storm. Be thankful when your sin troubles you, when it agitates you and makes you uneasy and keeps you awake at night. When that no longer happens, beware; for the sleep of indifference and of satisfaction in sin is all but fatal.

Having done everything that they could in the way of praying and in the way of navigation and in the

handling of the ship, and all to no avail, the captain
suddenly remembers the passenger who came aboard
at Joppa. "Where's that passenger who joined us
at Joppa?" They searched through the ship, and at
length came upon him sound asleep in his hiding
place in the sides of the vessel. Standing over him,
the captain shouts, "What meanest thou, O sleeper?
Is it possible that you can sleep on the brink of the
pit of death? Does it make no difference to you if
you perish, or if we perish? Arise and call upon thy
God, if so he will think upon us that we perish not.
We have tried our gods, but without success. Perhaps your God will hear you and save us."

Without waiting to see whether Jonah prayed or
not—and probably he did not, for he was not in a
praying mood, and was trying to get as far away as
possible from the face of the Lord, instead of coming
into his presence by prayer—the captain gathered
the crew of the ship to discover by lot who was responsible for the evil which had come upon them. It
was more than superstition this time, for there was
one in that ship's company because of whom the
great storm had arisen. Here we have a contrast
between Jonah in this famous voyage of the Old Testament and Paul in the famous voyage of the New
Testament. Because Paul was on the ship, the whole
ship's company was saved. "Lo, I have given thee,"
said the angel to Paul, "the lives of all them that sail

with thee." Here everyone's life is in jeopardy because Jonah is on board.

The lots are cast in the lap and the seamen gather around for the drawing of the lot. By the dim light of the swinging ship's lantern, you can see the anxiety stamped on every face. Each man's past, each man's sin, is making him say, "Lord, is it I?" Each one searched through his past. One thought of the merchant he had drowned in the harbor at Sidon. Another said, "That woman whom I robbed at the Piraeus." Another, "That girl whom I seduced in Egypt." Each one said to himself, "Is it I?" But when the lot came out it had Jonah's number on it. The lot fell on Jonah. This was just chance, you say. Yes, it was chance; but chance overruled by the determination of God. "The lot is cast in the lap, but the disposal thereof is of the Lord."

The captain now says to Jonah, "What is thy name? thy country? thy people? and what is thine occupation?" Just an innocent question, and a very natural one on the part of the navigator; but it must have pierced the breast of Jonah like a sword. "My occupation? Yes; the prophet's occupation! And here I am on this ship trying to flee from the face of the Lord, going down to death and carrying these innocent men down with me." That is a striking question, "What is thine occupation?" It will come at times when our location and our disposition are out of all keeping with our occupation. What is thine occupation? It is a good question for the minister to ask himself, and a good question for the Christian to ask himself. Does my life square with my occupation?

Suddenly brought to himself by this unexpected question, "What is thine occupation?" Jonah preaches a great sermon; his congregation these pagan seamen; his pulpit the pitching deck of the storm-driven ship; and for a choir the roar of the gale and the thunder of the waves. Paul once preached a sermon under similar circumstances, and a very similar sermon, too. Standing on the deck of his vessel, and just the same kind of a ship, and perhaps on the same part of the Mediterranean, Paul told the two hundred and seventy-six seamen, soldiers, and passengers that he was the servant of God, "whose I am and whom I serve," and that although the ship would be wrecked there would be no loss of life. Now Jonah declares that he is a Hebrew, that he fears the Lord the God of heaven, that he is a prophet of God, and had been sent to cry against Nineveh, but instead of doing so had tried to flee from the presence of the Lord. When the mariners heard this, they were afraid. They believed that it was because of him the storm had broken upon the ship, and yet since he was a prophet of the God of the Hebrews, what could they do to him, even if he had sinned?

They said to Jonah, "What will we do unto thee that the sea may be calm unto us?"

Now comes the great miracle of this book, far greater than the physical miracles of the great fish. It is the moral and spiritual regeneration of Jonah. He tells them plainly, "For my sake, this great tempest is upon you. Cast me into the sea, and the sea shall be calm unto you." This is a new and spiritual Jonah whom we see. In the first place, he acknowledges that his sin has brought the storm upon the ship. "For my sake." It is sad and profoundly true that no man sins to himself. Some influence goes out from every life, direct or indirect, by shadow, by voice, or by touch. So it was here. Jonah's rebellion and sin has involved all these mariners in peril. "For thy sake," God said to the man after the fall, "for thy sake, the ground is cursed." Then Jonah, who has confessed his sin, confessed also the justice of the divine punishment and retribution. He asks that they cast him into the sea. Such a spirit is always a true sign of conviction and repentance. With true penitence and confession there is always the acceptance of the divine penalty. However men may debate and discuss the subject of hell, hell never troubles the awakened and penitent sinner; that is, the justice of the punishment never troubles him. He is like the penitent thief on the Cross, who said to his mocking comrade, "We receive the due reward of our deeds." With true penitence, there goes also a deep desire to do some good for others and a willingness to make the supreme sacrifice itself. So here Jonah proposes that he be cast into the sea.

Jonah's confession and the brief sermon that he preached about his occupation and the God of the Hebrews had already had its effect on the minds of the mariners. They were touched by his proposal, and yet dreaded to lay hands upon a prophet of God. Therefore, they tried once again, laying hold of the oars, to bring the ship to the shore. But the waves rose higher than ever, and wilder was the roar of the gale. Then, reluctantly, and beseeching God that he would not hold against them as a crime and sin what they were about to do, and that they thought that they were carrying out the divine wish, they took up Jonah and heaved him over the side of the vessel into the raging deep. Immediately the sea ceased from her raging. Here we are dealing with more than a storm on the Mediterranean. We are dealing with storms in the breast of man. Sin brings on the storm. It may be calm without, on the surface; but within, underneath, there is the raging tempest. Confession and penitence alone bring peace. When sin is cast out and Christ comes in, then he can say to the storm, as he did once on Galilee, "Peace, be still." There is no rest to the wicked. They are like the waves of the sea which cannot be still, but cast up mire and dirt. Conscience heaves the soul as the tide heaves the ocean.

Delivered in a miraculous manner from death in the sea, Jonah, now safe on the land, lifts up his voice in one of the greatest prayers and thanksgivings of the Bible. "Salvation," he says, at the end of this great hymn and prayer, "is of the Lord." None knew it better than Jonah. Converted himself, Jonah is now ready to convert others. The word of the Lord came to Jonah *the second time.* A great verse that; and how Jonah must have rejoiced over that second chance! What if God spoke to us but once, and never again. But how many second chances he gives us in his patience and his mercy. Jonah fled, was cast into the sea, but the word of the Lord came to him the second time, "Go to Nineveh and preach." Peter denied his Lord and swore that he had never seen him, but by the shore of Galilee Jesus appeared to him *the second time* and said, "Feed my sheep." John Mark failed the first time when he turned back at Pamphylia, and Paul was angry and would have nothing to do with him. But later on in the Epistles, we hear Paul, a prisoner at Rome now, telling Timothy to come to Rome and to bring Mark with him, for "he is profitable to me in the ministry." The word of God came to Mark *the second time.*

At Nineveh Jonah was commanded to "preach the preaching that I bid thee." That is the whole question about preaching. Have we a preaching, a message that God had bidden us, or just our own fancies and desires? What a curious mixture, in the way of preaching, the columns of a Monday morning metropolitan newspaper reveal. Strange, different, contradictory. No one would imagine that there was a preaching that God had commanded the preacher. There is a preaching which is based on the Bible as the Word of God, and there is a preaching which is nothing more than an expression of human desire, experience, or aspiration. The former preaching can, if God so wills it, make men or cities repent; the latter never has and never can make a man or a city repent.

Nineveh shows the possibilities of the preaching which God bids us. Up and down through this great metropolis passed the Hebrew prophet with his brief and powerful sermon, "Yet forty days and Nineveh shall be overthrown!" This was his cry, to the beggars and lepers at the city's gates, to the traders and traffickers at the market places and bazaars, to the soldiers and generals as they rolled by in their chariots, to the ladies and princesses in their gardens by the tawny Tigris, to the priests at their bloody rites in the temples, and to the king upon his throne. "Forty days; and then, if ye repent not, destruction!"

And the people repented, from the king on his throne to the beggar on the dunghill. They put on sackcloth, even the very beasts, and humbled themselves before the Lord. For who can tell, said the king, if God will turn and repent and turn away from his fierce anger that we perish not. God saw their repentance and spared the city. His judgments are true and fearful; but his mercy is great, even as the petulant Jonah said, "I knew that thou art a gracious God, and merciful, slow to anger, and of great kindness, and repentest thee of the evil." Yes, Jonah was not quite ready for it, as the sequel of his anger and impatience shows; but there's a wideness in God's mercy like the wideness of the sea.

This is the greatest recorded triumph of preaching. A whole vast city, from the king to the beggar, all classes, all conditions, repent and turn from their sins to God and are spared. There is nothing like it in the history of preaching. Christ remembered it when he was met with the unbelief and the impenitence of the men of his day, for he said to them, "The men of Nineveh shall rise in judgment with this generation and shall condemn it: because they repented at the preaching of Jonah, and behold a greater than Jonah is here." That "greater than Jonah" was, and ever is, Christ himself. Christ singles out the preaching of Jonah as the most powerful and successful on record; and yet a greater than Jonah is here. Populations, times, desires, customs, fashions, change; but God's preaching goes on, the same yesterday, today, and forever. The preaching of the greatest of preachers has in it these two major chords, "repentance" and "forgiveness." Does ancient Nineveh condemn anyone here today? When you rise up in the judgment together with the Ninevites, will some citizen of Nineveh pass by you into Eternal Life because he repented at the preaching of Jonah, whereas you are still impenitent under the preaching of Christ? Jonah turned the men of Nineveh to a godly life. What effect is it having on your life, not the preaching of Jonah, but the preaching of him of whom Jonah was but the type. Jonah had only words to give to the men of Nineveh. "Yet forty days and Nineveh shall be destroyed." But Christ comes with more than words. He comes with the great Act of God's love and justice. He comes with himself, uplifted upon the Cross. He comes accompanied by the hosts of the redeemed, all those who heard the story of God's love, all those who saw him hanging upon the cross, and repented and believed and were saved.

XII. *Isaiah — The greatest Christian in the Old Testament*

PETER said that "holy men of old spake as they were moved by the Holy Ghost." This account of the origin of the books of the Old Testament occasions no difficulty in the case of the prophet Isaiah, for such noble and sublime utterance is difficult to account for save on the ground of divine inspiration. His music is not of the earth earthy, but such music as only heaven can produce.

John called Isaiah the man who saw Christ's glory before he came and spoke of him. Everywhere this glory of the coming Christ is reflected in the face of the Prophet Isaiah. "Abraham rejoiced," Christ said, "to see my day"; and "Moses," he said, "wrote of me." In the Psalms of David, too, Christ said his work of redemption was foretold. But more than Abraham, or Moses, or David, or any Old Testament character or writer, Isaiah is the man who saw the glory of Christ. Joseph we called the most Christian character of the Old Testament. By that we

[159]

meant that in his patience and purity and trust in the providence of God, and in his beautiful forgiveness of those who had cruelly wronged him, Joseph is the most Christlike man in the Old Testament. When we call Isaiah the greatest Christian in the Old Testament, we are thinking of something else; not his personal character and conduct, although, as we shall see, he was Christlike in that respect, but his knowledge of and appreciation of Christ as the Savior and Redeemer of the world, and his presentation of Christ in his work of atoning for sinners. No one is a Christian in the highest sense until he sees Christ as Isaiah described him in the fifty-third chapter, bearing our sins, wounded for our transgressions, and bruised for our iniquities.

This accounts for the fact that Isaiah is in the New Testament the most frequently quoted of all the Old Testament writers. When the New Testament wishes to say something great about Christ, about his birth, about his atoning death, about his kingdom and the glory of his church, it says it in the words of Isaiah. Jesus began his ministry in the synagogue at Nazareth, when he read the lesson for the day from the sixty-first chapter of Isaiah: "The spirit of the Lord is upon me, because he hath anointed me to preach the Gospel to the poor." And the last direct scriptural quotation by Jesus was at the Last Supper when he quoted the fifty-third chapter of Isaiah, "He was numbered with the transgressors," and said it was fulfilled in him. John the Baptist commenced his ministry with the music of Isaiah, "Prepare ye the way of the Lord, make his paths straight"; and the last words of St. Paul as a preacher are the words he quoted in his prison at Rome from the prophecy of Isaiah.

Of all the books of the Old Testament, we could least afford to lose the book of Isaiah, for there we have the Gospel before Christ came to preach it and to seal it with his blood. From this book the people of God in every generation have found precious promises to sustain them on their pilgrim journey through this world. There they have seen Christ in all the pathos of his suffering, uplifted for sinners on the Cross. There they have rested beside softly flowing waters, and in the shadow of a great rock, and have trusted in the Lord of the way. There they have stood in peaceful and beautiful Beulah Land, and, like the pilgrims in John Bunyan's allegory, have seen the glory of the city toward which they are traveling.

The great verses and promises of the book of Isaiah would make a Bible in themselves. What would we do without them? Here are just a few of them: "With joy shall ye draw water out of the wells of salvation"; "Seek ye the Lord while he may be found. Call upon him when he is near"; "Thou wilt keep him in perfect peace whose mind is stayed on thee"; "He will swallow up death in victory";

"The Lord God will wipe away tears from off all faces"; "Eye hath not seen nor ear heard, neither have entered into the mind of man the things which God hath prepared for them that love him"; "Thine eye shall see the King in his beauty"; "The ransomed of the Lord shall return with songs and everlasting joy upon their head"; "Comfort ye, comfort ye my people, said your God"; "He shall feed his flocks like a shepherd; he shall carry the lambs with his arms"; "They that wait upon the Lord shall renew their strength. They shall mount up with wings as eagles"; "When thou passeth through the waters, I will be with thee; and through the rivers they shall not overflow"; "I have graven thee on the palms of my hands"; "Surely he hath borne our griefs and carried our sorrows"; "Ho, everyone that thirsteth; come ye to the waters"; "Though your sins be as scarlet, they shall be as wool; though they be red like crimson, they shall be as white as snow." Yes, take away every book of the Old Testament, but leave us Isaiah, with his "wild, seraphic fire." The best way to understand the language of heaven and fit ourselves for citizenship in the city of God is to know the music of Isaiah. "Silver tones of which the ear is never weary, honeyed rhetoric which thrills like a subtle odor those who have lost the key to its meaning."

There are two classes of great men—those who are great in action, and those who are great in thought and utterance. Most of the Old Testament heroes of whom we have been speaking thus far were men who were great in action; although some of them, like Moses and David, were great both in action and in thought. Isaiah belongs to the second class. He does appear, indeed, as a striking and powerful actor in one scene of the drama of Hebrew history; but for the most part he is a man who is great in thought and utterance. Of some of those who were greatest in thought and utterance, such as Homer and Shakespeare, we know almost nothing; yet what they said and what they thought is the heritage of mankind. We know very little about the life of Isaiah. He was the son of Amoz, a man of priestly line and training. Called with an overwhelming vision to prophesy to the people, he lived through the reigns of four kings, appears in a great national crisis as the deliverer of his people, and then passes from our view. Hebrew tradition describes him as one of the victims of the wicked reign of Manasseh, the son and successor to Hezekiah. He was thrust into a hollow tree, and when he refused to recant or to acknowledge any transgression, was sawn asunder. Hebrews 11:37, "They were sawn asunder," is supposed to refer to the martyr death of the great prophet.

The call of Isaiah came in the reign of the great King Uzziah, in some respects the greatest of the Hebrew kings after David. Isaiah dismisses his natural birth with a single sentence; but he has much to say about his second birth, when he saw the Lord. That is the real birthday that a man ought to celebrate. Uzziah had conquered the enemies of Israel, the Philistines, the Arabians, and the Ammonites. With his regular army of three hundred thousand men, military towers and depots, and engines which he had invented, he was feared clear to the gates of Egypt. Then came the tragedy of his fall. Man is not made for too much power or too much popularity. When he was at the height of his splendor and glory, Uzziah, in an evil moment, went to the temple to offer the sacrifice, thus arrogating to himself the holy office of the priest. Repulsed at the sacred threshhold by the priests, Uzziah was overcome with rage and was about to smite the priests, when lo, he became a leper white as snow. The last days of the great monarch were spent in a lazar house, with none too poor to do him honor. How God brings down the mighty from their seats and exalts the humble!

It was in the year that the great king died that Isaiah went up to the Temple. Perhaps he had just come from the funeral of the once mighty monarch. The glory and power of Israel seemed to have departed. But just when the glory of man had faded from his vision, the glory of God is revealed unto Isaiah. Here in the temple he heard the music of the four hundred chanting Levites; here his eyes rested upon the familiar but sublime objects—tables, incense, lamps, veils, and cherubim. Then suddenly came the Reality, of which all these things were the symbols. "I saw the Lord."

Great lives often draw their inspiration and power and endurance from one experience of God. This was true of Moses, who looked back to his burning bush and spoke of it at the very end of his life. It was true of St. Paul, who ever looked back to the day when he saw the Lord outside the gates of Damascus. The experience upon which Isaiah draws through the forty years of his great ministry was this vision of the glory of God in the temple at Jerusalem. "I saw the Lord sitting upon a throne."

The first effect of this overwhelming vision was to impress Isaiah with his own sinfulness. The glory of God revealed Isaiah unto himself. If you measure yourself by others, and by yourself, you will have little cause for anxiety. It is when you stand in the presence of the infinite holiness that you cry out, as Peter did in the fishing smack when he fell at the feet of Jesus, "Depart from me, O Lord, for I am a sinful man!" When Isaiah had seen the glory of God in the temple, he cried out, "Woe is me, for I am undone, for I am a man of unclean lips, and mine eyes have seen the King, the Lord of hosts." Wherever the church drifts from the true Gospel and from Jesus Christ as a Redeemer from sin, and feeds itself with the husks of this world, the reason is that the sense of sin has faded. Unless man is a sinner, he does not

need Christ as a Savior. The Cross in all its majesty
and glory has meaning for a sinner only. Those who
have felt and expressed to the utmost the glory and
power of Christ as a Redeemer and Savior are men
like Isaiah, Peter, John, and Paul, who knew themselves to be the chief of sinners.

First came the vision of God; then the vision of
self as a sinner; and now comes the vision of duty
and of opportunity. Swift as Isaiah confessed his
sin, one of the sublime creatures, the seraphim, flew
to him and touched his lips with a coal from off the
altar as a sign that his iniquity was taken away.
Then Isaiah hears the Voice, "Whom shall I send,
and who will go for us?" Immediately he answers,
"Here am I; send me." So Paul said when he saw
the glory of God, "Lord, what wilt thou have me to
do?" Henceforth, the work of Isaiah is to speak the
word of the Lord to the people of Israel. God might
have employed archangels or seraphim to proclaim
forgiveness to sinners, but instead of that he has
chosen forgiven sinners like Isaiah and Peter and
John and Paul. Since redemption was wrought for
sinners, the story of God's love can be told by a forgiven sinner more eloquently, more tenderly, more
persuasively, than by an angel himself.

In the days of Hezekiah and Sennacherib, Isaiah
appears not only as the teacher and prophet of
Israel, but as a national deliverer. When Hezekiah
received the impious threat of the Assyrian despot

who railed at the God of Israel, he went to the temple and spread the letter out before the Lord. But he also sent a messenger unto Isaiah. In sublime and magnificent language Isaiah defies Sennacherib, the master of the world, telling him that God will defend the city and save it for the sake of David, his servant. "Because thy rage against me and thy tumult is come up into mine ears, therefore will I put my hook in thy nose and my bridle in thy lips, and I will turn thee back by the way which thou camest." The rest of the story is told in these words: "Then the angel of the Lord went forth and smote in the camp of the Assyrians a hundred and fourscore and five thousand, and when they arose early in the morning, behold they were all dead corpses." Isaiah and his trust in the Lord God of Israel had received a magnificent vindication. In the national crisis the man of God was the man of the hour. In the crisis and distress under which our nation labors today, we have all kinds of experts—financial, industrial, social, economic; but in public life we do not hear the accents of the man of God. The great need of the nation and of the world is to recover spiritual and moral values. A man like Isaiah is worth more to a nation than an army and navy.

The greatest thing about Isaiah was his witness to Christ. "He saw his glory and spoke of him." He is called the "evangelical" prophet, because more than any of the prophets or patriarchs Isaiah saw the glory of Christ on the Cross. It is not necessary to listen long to the sermon or to the prayer or to the speech of the preacher to know whether or not he belongs to the order of the evangelical prophets and proclaims the great truths of sin and grace. Preachers and teachers there are who are other than evangelical. They have their day, their sway, and their popularity, and, to popular view, may seem often to eclipse in significance the evangelical prophet. But in the long look, the great messengers of God are prophets of the evangelical order, they who proclaim to mankind the redeeming grace of God in Jesus Christ his Son. To do that, to bear witness unto him, Christ established his Church in the world; and wherever that witness is not made, there you may have large congregations, beautiful music, noble architecture, chaste eloquence, and persuasive speech; but not the true Church which is the power and the wisdom of God unto salvation.

The witness of Isaiah to Christ is best summed up in one great chapter, the fifty-third. Moses, David, Peter, John, and Paul—all glory in the Cross of Christ. But when we wish to look upon the most moving pictures of the Crucifixion, and listen to the most moving and uplifting music of redemption, it is to Isaiah that we go. There we behold, first of all, the despised and rejected Christ. "He was despised and rejected of men." The world often praises Christ as a leader, as a prophet, as a teacher, as an example. Christ cares nothing for that. What he wants to know is what the world thinks of him as the Savior of sinners. Still, in that office, men despise him and reject him and turn away their faces from him.

Here, too, we behold the dying and the atoning Christ, the sin-bearer, who hath borne our griefs and carried our sorrows, wounded for our transgressions and bruised for our iniquities. Just how or why that could be, we cannot tell. The angels themselves desire to look into that. All we can say is that "all we like sheep have gone astray, and the Lord hath laid on him the iniquity of us all."

Here, too, we behold the risen, ascended, and triumphant Savior. "He shall prolong his days. He shall see of the travail of his soul and be satisfied. Therefore, will I divide him a portion with the great, and he shall divide a portion with the strong, because he hath poured out his soul unto death." Others founded their kingdoms on their conquests, or their riches, their cruelties. Their kingdoms have passed. Christ founded his kingdom upon his death. It abides forever. Napoleon, standing on his rock prison on the South Atlantic, said, and truly: "I die before my time. My body will be given back to the earth to be done with as men please, and to become the food of worms. Such will be the fate of him who has been called the great Napoleon. What an abyss between my deep misery and the eternal

Kingdom of Christ, which is proclaimed, loved, and adored, and is extending over the whole earth."

We need this note of triumph in the church today. Everywhere we behold what looks like a revival of paganism. The beast of the Apocalypse emerges again out of the abyss with his death stroke healed; and again the world follows the beast and worships him and wonders at him. Where, you ask, are the signs of the victory and conquest of Christ and his kingdom? Where do we stand now in the long night of watching and waiting? Is it the first, the second, the third, or the fourth watch? The last watch will be the longest and the hardest, when the night is deepest, when physical energies are at their lowest ebb, and a gray breath creeps over men and things, aging them. Yet, as Christ came once at the fourth watch over storm-swept Gennesareth, so he will come to his Church. "He shall see of the travail of his soul and be satisfied." "He shall not rest or be weary till he have set justice in the earth."

All this I see. All this I hear when I read the pages of the prophet Isaiah, who saw Christ's glory and spoke of him. I see the kingdom of Satan overthrown. But I see something more than that. I see Christ as the sinner's Savior, my own Redeemer; and all my hope will be based upon what Isaiah, who saw his glory, said of him, "Though your sins be as scarlet, they shall be as wool; though they be red like crimson, they shall be as white as snow."

"Tell me, I pray thee, all the great things
that Elisha hath done."   II KINGS 8: 4.

XIII. *Elisha — The greatest pastor in the Old Testament*

THAT must have been an
interesting story that Gehazi, the servant of Elisha,
told to Joram, the king of Israel. Not only interesting, but thrilling; for no man had more interesting
experiences than Elisha. More striking incidents
are related of him than of any other character of
the Old Testament. More familiar proverbs, too,
such as the Prophet's Chamber, the Widow's Cruse
of Oil, the Mantle of Elijah, the School of the
Prophets, "I dwell among mine own people," are associated with Elisha than with any other man of the
Old Testament. When Christ asked his disciples
whom men took him to be, they answered that some
thought he was Elijah. But in many respects Elisha
was more like Christ than Elijah. He had in him
more of the human, the gentle, and the domestic than
his mighty predecessor. With one or two exceptions,
the numerous miracles which he worked were deeds
of mercy and of kindness. In this respect he was a

forerunner of Christ, for like Christ he went about doing good. His name, Elisha, has a softer sound than Elijah; and when you proceed from the history of Elijah to that of Elisha it is like coming down from the gaunt and naked mountains into the rolling plains. It is not the voice of the whirlwind and the earthquake that one hears when Elisha speaks, but the "still, small voice."

I call him the greatest pastor of the Old Testament; and that not only on the record of his life, but upon the testimony of his contemporaries, for he was known as "the man of God." The Shunammite woman so described him to her husband: "I perceive that this is an holy man of God which passeth by us continually."

The great day in a pastor's life is the day of his ordination. A sacredness and beauty gather around that solemn act when by the laying on of hands, which goes clear back to the days of St. Paul and Timothy, the young man is set apart to the Gospel ministry. Elisha's ordination was unique. It was springtime in the valley of the Jordan. The trees were putting forth their leaves; the time for the singing of birds had come; and the voice of the turtle was heard in the land. On the farm of Shaphat, all the hired hands were out plowing, and Shaphat's son, Elisha, was with them, following the twelve yoke of oxen as they dragged the wooden plows through the alluvial soil of the fertile Jordan Valley. Suddenly, Elijah steps up behind Elisha and throws his mantle over his shoulders. Elisha understood at once the significance of the act. The east sets great store by the mantle of the preacher and the prophet. In one of the mosques at Konia, Turkey, the Iconium of St. Paul and the book of Acts, I saw the turban and the robes of celebrated Moslem rulers and teachers, the founders of the order of the dervishes. Elisha asked permission to go and kiss his father. Thus, at the very beginning of Elisha's history, the note of domesticity and of the affections of the home is struck. But when he bade his parents farewell, Elisha sacrificed the oxen and their instruments as a token of his complete devotion to Elijah and to the Words of the Lord.

Elisha was God's answer to the prayer of the despondent Elijah beneath the juniper tree, "I am not better than my fathers. It is enough, O Lord; take away my life." Elijah thought that all his labors were in vain and that God's cause was doomed; but all the while God was preparing Elisha to be the successor of Elijah. So today on the hillsides, following the plow as it turns up the moist soil, or rollicking on the college campuses, or working in the factory, are the young men upon whom God will lay his hand, and who are to be the preachers, the prophets, the teachers, and the leaders of tomorrow.

Elisha had a grand ordination. It came from none other than the hand of Elijah. But after a pastor has been ordained and duly charged, the next thing

is to see what he will say. What is the message of
Elisha? "The voice said, What shall I cry?" Elisha
does not leave us long in doubt as to that. The time
has come for Elijah to be translated. He desired to
pass out of the world alone, for alone he had lived.
But Elisha will not let him do that. He accompanies
him over the parted Jordan, asks for a double portion
of Elijah's spirit, and then, beholding him swept up
into heaven with the whirlwind and the chariot and
horses of fire, pronounces the great eulogy on Elijah,
"My father, my father! The chariot of Israel and
the horseman thereof." Then he took up the fallen
mantle of Elijah and commenced his prophetic career
which was to last for more than half a century.

> "God of the prophets, bless the prophet's sons;
> Elijah's mantle o'er Elisha cast."

When he came down to the Jordan, Elisha took
the mantle of Elijah, and crying out, "Where is the
God of Elijah?" smote the waters. The parted
waters were the answer to his prayer and his test.
"Where is the God of Elijah?" Elisha knew what
the God of Elijah had been able to do. He could ask
for nothing better than that. He had no new message, no new God that he has discovered; but goes
forth to teach and to heal and to preach in the Name
of the God of Elijah.

"Where is the God of Elijah?" We know what
the God of Elijah and the God of John and the

God of Paul has been able to do; we know what the Gospel of redemption, the faith once for all delivered to the saints has done; how it has lifted empires off their hinges and turned the rivers of history into new channels; how it was the salt that has kept cities and civilizations from corruption; how it has transformed lives and communities, turned the blasphemer into the apostle, the thief into the preacher, brought light and hope to uncounted souls, founded institutions of mercy and healing, and sent the Christian pilgrim singing on his way to prison and to death. Before we abandon that Gospel, let us be sure that we have a better one. Before we throw away the mantle of Elijah and Peter and John and Paul, let us be sure that we have another garment with which we can work these miracles.

Elisha made no boast of having discovered a new God. His message was the old message of repentance and righteousness. The preacher is not an explorer, a discoverer, an inventor, but a herald. He comes in the Name of God. In that sense, every pastor can be a great preacher because he has a great message to proclaim. Joseph Parker and Charles H. Spurgeon were contemporaries and the chief luminaries of the pulpits of London. One who went to hear both of them preach made this comment: "Parker made me feel that he was a great man. Spurgeon made me feel that Jesus is a great Savior."

Elisha was also an educator. He was president of

a theological seminary, head of the School of the Prophets. He had the long vision and knew that his own work was not enough. What he did would be multiplied by training other young men for the prophetic office. That is always the duty and the privilege of the pastor. The most successful of them must know that he cannot last long, that others must take up the message and repeat it when his voice is quenched in death. So Elisha spent much time at the School of the Prophets. Theological seminaries are fountains of blessing and inspiration, as long as they are true to the Bible and true to the Gospel. When they depart from that, then it would be difficult to imagine a greater blight or curse. When seminaries send men out into the church and into the world to say, "Hath God said?" rather than, "Thus saith the Lord," the sooner they are destroyed the better.

Elisha was a public benefactor. Most of his miracles are miracles of helpfulness and blessing in the ordinary processes of life. When the pot of soup out of which the young theologians were eating in the refectory was poisoned by the gourds, Elisha healed it with the antidote of meal which he cast into the pot. That is the privilege and the opportunity of the pastor, to heal the death in the pot; the death in the pot of many of the popular philosophies, theories, practices, and the literature of the day. The meal with which he can do it is the truth of God's Word.

Elijah made iron swim. On a spring day the sons of the prophets went out to build a more commodious dormitory. They were felling trees for the logs, and as one of them fetched a great blow, the ax head flew off into the river. "Alas, my master!" cried the young prophet, "What shall I do?" Elisha had him point out the spot, and thrusting in a stick, "the iron did swim." In a figurative sense, that is what the pastor must ever try to do. He must try to make iron swim. He sees souls about him all the time into whom the iron has entered, the iron of sorrow, or sickness and suffering, or sin and transgression. His work is to make the iron swim, to turn adversity into blessing, to bring good out of evil, to turn dross into gold.

Jericho was attractively situated. "The situation of the city," one of its inhabitants said, "is pleasant; but the water is naught, and the land barren." Elisha took a cruse full of salt and cast it into the spring of waters, and henceforth they were healed. This is a picture of many a city of our day—the situation is pleasant, but the springs of its life are poisoned. Pittsburgh is a city pleasant for situation, with the great hills rising all about it, and the historic rivers mingling here their waters as they flow to the south. Fairest of all is the city at night, where magic lights glow on river, on hillside, and in the midst of the city, answering the stars of heaven. Yet how many of its springs are poisoned! As in every city, so here, the springs of political life are poisoned. Fountains of gambling, drinking, oppression, stealing, licentiousness, day and night pour forth their poisoned waters. Only one thing can heal it. No secular education, nor mandates from the city hall; but the salt of the Gospel. Therefore, preacher, teacher, parent, friend of man, wherever thou art, throw in the salt. Someone's drink shall be healed thereby, and the land shall cease to be barren.

Elisha was at his best in the home. There we see him in his compassion and friendly sympathetic interest. There was a poor widow and a godly woman, too, whose husband had been one of the sons of the prophets. Death came along and took him off. Then depression came; the family was heavily in debt. Debt is always bad, but it was a more serious thing then. The creditor came along one day to take the widow's two sons in place of the money she owed. Elisha asked her what was in the house. Not anything save a pot of oil. He told her to borrow vessels of all her neighbors. "Borrow not a few." At his direction, she set the vessels up in her house, and taking the pot of oil, began to pour into the empty vessels. When they were all full, the oil stayed. Then the woman took the oil, sold it, paid her debts, and lived happily the rest of her days. Thus the widow's cruse of oil has become a proverb which means the providential care and goodness of God.

One of the chief rewards of the pastor is to be able to bless a home.

Another home which Elisha blessed was that of the woman of Shunem. A "great woman," she is called, and worthy of the title. Elisha was often entertained in their home when he came to preach in the church at Shunem. One day she said to her husband, "Behold, now, I perceive that this is an holy man of God which passeth by us continually. Let us make a little chamber, I pray thee, on the wall, and let us set for him there a bed and a table and a stool and a candlestick, and it shall be, when he cometh to us, that he shall turn in thither." It was a chamber on the wall, with its door opening on the outside, so that Elisha could come and go as he passed. Hence the name that persists to this day, "the prophet's chamber," the room where the pastor is entertained.

One day a child was born to this woman of Shunem. When he was old enough to walk about by himself, he followed the men out to the fields at the harvest season. There he suffered a sunstroke and cried out to his father, "My head, my head!" The father did what he could for him, and then said what all fathers must say, "Carry him to his mother." But even his mother could do nothing. At noon, as he lay in her arms, the child died. The mother then took him and laid him on the bed of the man of God, and rode off to Mount Carmel where Elisha was staying that time.

When he learned her agony, Elisha first sent his servant with his staff. But when Gehazi laid the staff on the face of the dead child, "there was neither voice nor hearing." The indirect method was not successful. Then Elisha came in person, and going up to the prophet's chamber, stretched himself upon the child. When the child revived, he called to the woman and said to her, "Take up thy child." She must have felt the way the wife of Jairus did when Jesus restored her little daughter, or the way the widow of Nain did when Jesus gave her back her son.

Elisha knew how to deal with sinners. When Naaman, the great man of Syria, came to be healed of his leprosy, Elisha sent him a brief message to go down and wash seven times in the Jordan. Naaman was enraged at what he took to be a slight. He thought that so great a man should be dealt with in a different way. "Behold," he said, "I thought he would surely come out to me and stand and call on the name of the Lord his God and strike his hand over the place and recover the leper. Are not Abana and Pharpar, rivers of Damascus, better than all the waters of Israel? May I not wash in them and be clean?" So he turned and went away in a rage. The plain message of the Gospel is this—"Wash and be clean." That is a message which cannot be softened, toned down, or adulterated; and like the message that Elisha gave to Naaman the leper, is a message of mercy and kindness.

The secret of Elisha's power was his contact with the unseen world. He was able to look at the things which are not seen. He was conscious of another order than this present order of things. When the Syrian army had him surrounded on his mountain at Dothan, his servant was in despair and cried out, "What shall we do?" Elisha said to him, "Fear not, for they that be with us are more than they that be with them." And Elisha prayed and said, "Lord, I pray thee, open his eyes that he may see." And the Lord opened the eyes of the young man and he saw, and behold the mountain was full of horses and chariots of fire round about Elisha. That is the high office of the preacher and the pastor—to open the eyes of the young man to what is seen only with the eye of faith; to impress him with the reality and existence of a spiritual world; to let him know that life is more than meat and drink and sex, and that by faith he becomes the inhabitant of a spiritual empire. "Thousands of spiritual beings walk abroad, both when we wake and when we sleep." One day our eyes shall be opened, and we shall see how that world is the reality, and this but the shadow.

Others in the Bible worked great miracles, but Elisha is the only man who worked a miracle from his grave. Sometime after his death a funeral procession was on its way to the cemetery. Suddenly a band of invading Moabites made their appearance. Unable to reach the prepared grave, the bearers cast the man into the sepulcher of Elisha; and when he touched the bones of Elisha he revived and stood on his feet. The influence of a good man, and especially a good pastor and minister, goes on after his death; even from his grave he continues to speak. His sepulcher is a pulpit. Speaking of his godly mother, Thomas Carlyle said, "From your grave yonder in Ecclefechan churchyard you bid him trust in God, and that he will still try to do." Yes; what can be more real or more potent than the influence of godly men and women whose voice is no longer heard and whose face is no longer seen? He being dead yet speaketh. "Blessed are the dead which die in the Lord from henceforth: Yea, saith the Spirit, that they may rest from their labors, and their works do follow them."

"Moses, whom the Lord knew face to face."

DEUTERONOMY 34: 10.

XIV. *Moses—The man over whose body heaven and hell fought*

GOD spake with Moses face to face. That will ever be his highest distinction. God came into closer fellowship with Moses than with any man since the Fall. To tell the story of Moses is to tell the story of divine revelation, of the redeeming purpose, and the history of a race. A whole nation, with a great past and a mighty future, exists as a monument to Moses.

The imprint of Moses on the ages is reflected in the inspired and uninspired stories of what happened to him at his death. The place of his burial was secret; evidently, lest the people should worship Moses instead of God. St. Jude has a strange passage in which he tells us that the archangel Michael and the devil contended one with the other over the possession of the body of Moses. He was so great a man that heaven and hell fought over his body. A Jewish legend relates that when the angel of death was sent to take away the soul of Moses, he was overcome with the majesty of the prophet and withdrew from him in fear. None of the angels in heaven was mighty enough to take away the soul of Moses. Therefore, God drew his soul from him with a kiss. That beautiful tradition illustrates at once the grandeur of Moses, that majesty which is reflected in Michelangelo's famous statue in the Church of St. Peter in Chains at Rome, and the favor with which God looked upon him.

The world will never develop itself or educate itself beyond the influence of a great man. Great men are the levers with which God moves the world. He can use for his purposes both good men and bad men, true prophets and false prophets, for he can make the wrath of man to praise him. The state of the world today, with dictators in Russia, Germany, Italy, and Turkey, is a striking illustration of the sway and influence of one man.

I. Moses and the Plan of God

The first thing that strikes us about Moses is the place which he occupied in the plan and purpose of God. Men are never great in themselves, but only in relationship to the plan of God, and as the instruments of his purpose. In the great plan of God for the redemption of the world, a plan which stretches from Abraham to Christ, from the calling of a man and a family to the death of Christ on the Cross, Moses is the chief link. God's plan is still marching on. Perhaps it is easier for us to realize that when we look back than when we look around us or in front of us. But still his eternal purposes advance irresistibly to their appointed goal. In the storms and confusions of our time, it is comforting and inspiring to remember this.

> "Our lives with various scenes are drawn,
> And vexed with trifling cares,
> While Thine eternal thought moves on
> Thine undisturbed affairs."

The providence of God in the life of Moses was strikingly present in the incidents attending his birth and infancy. Herod, in order to kill Jesus, issued his decree for the slaughter of the children of two years and under. Thus he thought to stop the plan of God. But Pharaoh outdid Herod in his cruelty and issued a decree that all male children of the Jews should be strangled at birth. But Moses records, "The midwives feared God and did not as the king of Egypt commanded them, but saved the men children alive." The fear of God in the heart of a nurse frustrates the might and wrath of the potentate of the world. In the contest with God, Herod and Pharaoh always lose.

The next decree was that every male child should be cast into the river Nile and drowned. Thus Pharaoh thought to circumvent the loyal and God-fearing conduct of the nurses. But when this child was born

in the home of Amram and Jochebed, and it was seen
that he was a goodly child, his mother hid him for
three months. Then, when it was no longer possible
to conceal him in the home, he was put in an ark of
bulrushes and laid in the flags by the river's brink,
while his sister, Miriam, stood afar off to see what
should be done. And this was what was done. The
daughter of Pharaoh came down to bathe in the Nile
and saw the child in his cradle in the bulrushes floating in the river. Josephus, the Jewish historian, adds
that this daughter of Pharaoh was married, but child-
less, and that she greatly desired children. As a result of this apparently chance meeting between the
daughter of the Egyptian king, whose decree had
gone forth for the death of this child, Moses was
saved from destruction and adopted into the family
of Pharaoh's daughter. The river which Pharaoh
had decreed was to destroy the child was the means
of his preservation. The maternal longing in the
breast of Pharaoh's daughter frustrated the monarch's cruel decree. Here certainly, if ever, we can
see the hand of God in history. Suppose that the
daughter of Pharaoh on that cloudless morning had
come down with her maidens to bathe in the river at
a point one hundred yards up or down the river from
where Moses lay in his cradle. Or suppose that she
had chosen to come on some other day and at some
other place. The whole thing looks like chance.
So far as the daughter of Pharaoh and Moses and

Miriam were concerned, it was chance. But in the providence of God events happened exactly as they did, and he who was to overthrow Egypt's hosts and deliver the people of God was thus preserved.

Life to you and me looks like a series of chance happenings, haphazard events, with no designing hand or planning mind. But there is a deeper meaning to life than this. God's hand is upon us. He knows the way that we take. We may choose our path, but the Lord directeth our feet. There is a divinity which is ever at work, shaping our ends, rough hew them how we will. The acknowledgment of this sublime truth gives you an anchor amid the storms and vicissitudes of your life.

II. THE CHOICE OF MOSES

Moses was educated as a son of Pharaoh's daughter; and Stephen said in his great speech in the Sanhedrin, before he was stoned to death, that Moses was "learned in all the wisdom of the Egyptians." We know today that the chief field of that Egyptian wisdom was death and its machinery, and the journeys and experiences that follow death. Very strange, therefore, that this man Moses, learned in all the lore of the Egyptians, when he comes to write his books and record his laws for the guidance of the Hebrew nation, leaves out entirely the subject of the future life. The only way in which to account for this is that the man who wrote these books and recorded these laws was divinely inspired of God.

Egyptian philosophy and life at the court did not spoil Moses. Stephen says that "it came into the heart of Moses to visit his brethren." He made a visit to Goshen, where the Hebrews lived, and when he saw an Egyptian abusing a Hebrew, Moses smote the Egyptian and slew him. Henceforth, he risks everything for the sake of his people. This is the fact which admits Moses into the New Testament's Hall of Fame. "By faith Moses, when he was come to years, refused to be called the son of Pharaoh's daughter, choosing rather to suffer afflictions with the people of God than to enjoy the pleasures of sin for a season, esteeming the reproach of Christ greater riches than the treasures in Egypt, for he had respect unto the recompense of the reward."

Moses was one of those who had the vision and the power of will to deny the present world for the sake of another world. The splendors of the Egyptian court were nothing to Moses compared with the suffering and afflictions with the people of God. Not all were able or willing to make this choice. The world and the church can advance only through the leadership of those who are willing to make the choice of Moses. They endure, and cause others to endure, because they see Him who is invisible.

Moses renounced the pleasures of sin for a season. Sin must have its pleasures and satisfactions, else there would not be so many sinners. But these pleasures are "for a season" only. They are quickly gone, like the snow on the face of the desert. Yet multitudes today, as always, are making that choice. Infatuated with the pleasure of the moment, after a little they all learn the folly of their choice and see the pleasures of sin turn to misery and unhappiness; whereas, the reproach of Christ becomes the smile of God. Every soul is placed upon the arena of life and is asked to choose. They who choose as Moses did are the immortal ones. Somewhere in some huge cavern, or in the heart of some sand-buried pyramid, there is a coffin in which molders the mummy of that forgotten Pharaoh who ruled Egypt in the day of Moses; whereas, the Hebrew boy whom his edict would have doomed to destruction lives forever.

III. The Burning Bush

Moses had chosen affliction with the people of God and already had struck a blow for their deliverance. But the call of God came forty years later, when the bush burned in the desert. All through the subsequent life of Moses he walks in the light of that burning bush. He hears wherever he goes the sound of that Voice which broke the stillness of the desert.

The life of Moses as a prophet and a deliverer illustrates the power of a single experience of the presence of God. One such experience is enough to animate and inspire and strengthen and safeguard through a long life. Moses had his burning bush; Samuel, the voice of God while he slept in the holy house at Shiloh; Isaiah, his vision of the cherubim in the temple; Paul, his vision and voice and burning light on the way to Damascus. Henceforth, all of them followed the light and obeyed the voice.

The burning bush was a striking, unforgettable sign and experience. Yet, to a certain extent, although in a different way, there is a bush that burns for all of us; and some little radiance, at least, all of us have caught from that bush, and life's most sacred memories gather about the bush. You know best when it was and what it was in your life. Perhaps it was a deep conviction, a strong urge to do good, and to serve God in your generation. Perhaps it was a light that kindled in the still countenance of a loved one who had passed through the gates of death. Perhaps it was a light and a voice that came to you in the midst of some great trial or sorrow. But whatever and wherever it was, you recognize it now as something different and apart from the common territory of life and the ordinary experiences of life. Moses was faithful to that desert experience. Even at the very end in his farewell to the people of Israel, he spoke of "the good will of him that dwelt in the bush." Have you been faithful to your voice, to your experience? If you have not, then now is the time to find your way back to the bush and renew your vows, ere the holy light goes out.

IV. The Disappointment and Death of Moses

After forty years of magnificent leadership, and complete devotion to Israel, Moses finished his work. The forty years of wandering are over, and the people are encamped tribe by tribe, standard by standard, around the ark on the borders of Canaan, ready to pass over the river Jordan. There lay the goal of all the dreams and all the labors of Moses. This was the good land toward which for forty years he had been leading his people. Yet the great leader is not permitted to pass over with the people.

On the borders of the Promised Land Moses remembers the word of God, spoken long ago, that he was not to go over the Jordan into the Promised Land. Yet when he saw the land before him, Moses made his pathetic petition that he might be permitted to go over with the people. "I pray thee, let me go over and see the good land that is beyond Jordan, that goodly mountain and Lebanon." But the Lord said to him, "Let it suffice thee. Speak no more unto me of this matter. Get thee up unto the top of Pisgah, and lift up thine eyes westward and northward and southward and eastward and behold it with thine eyes, for thou shalt not go over the Jordan."

The offense which now arises out of the past and stands like a barrier in the way of Moses happened at Kadesh, when he smote the rock to bring water out of the rock for the people. Wearied with the mur-

murings of the people on the occasion, Moses in a moment of impatience and loss of self-control exclaimed, "Hear, ye rebels; must I bring water for you out of the rock?" Then he lifted his rod and smote the rock, not once, but twice. His transgression, that of arrogating to himself the power to bring water out of the rock, and the anger which he displayed, strikes us as a not very serious offense, when we take into consideration the long record of faithfulness, obedience, and tender solicitude for his people, a devotion so sincere that on one occasion when he prayed for the forgiveness of the people, he asked God that if he would not forgive them, to blot his name out of the Book of Life. But if the offense strikes you and me as trivial and as a failing which leaned to virtue's side, that only goes to show the difference between man and God, and how his ways are not our ways, nor our thoughts his thoughts. A very searching and solemn commentary this is; the shutting out of Moses from the land of promise, upon the influence and far-reaching effect of a single sin. After the love of God, sin is the most powerful thing in the universe.

> "Moses, the man of meekest heart,
>   Lost Canaan by self will;
> To show where Grace has done its part,
>   How sin defiles us still."

Almost unsurpassed in the Scriptures is that final scene. No longer opposing the will of God, Moses climbed Mount Nebo to the top of Pisgah. From that lofty summit he surveyed the whole territory of Canaan. Beneath him flowed the river Jordan, to the north the Sea of Galilee, and to the south the Dead Sea. Where the mountains begin to rise on the other side lay Jericho with its palm trees, and in the distance the summit upon which the temple at Jerusalem was afterward to rise, and near it the Mount of Olives. Far to the northwest, Mount Tabor; and furthest in the distance, Mount Carmel; and beyond that, a flash of the Great Sea itself. Moses drew it all in like an inhalation. There was the land to which he had led his people, where their immortal destiny for the redemption of mankind was to be worked out, the land which was to be trodden by the sacred feet of Him of whom Moses wrote. But only with his eyes did Moses enter that land. "So Moses the servant of the Lord died there, and he buried him in a valley in the land of Moab over against Beth-Peor. But no man knoweth of his sepulcher unto this day."

> "By Nebo's lonely mountain,
>   On this side Jordan's wave,
> In a vale in the land of Moab,
>   There lies a lonely grave.
> And no man knows that sepulcher,
>   And no man saw it e'er,
> For the angels of God upturned the sod,
>   And laid the dead man there." [1]

[1] *The Burial of Moses*, C. F. Alexander.

But now the ages have passed and He of whom Moses wrote has come. Jesus with three of the disciples has climbed to the top of a mountain in that land. There he was transfigured in glory; and two men, Moses and Elijah, appeared with him in glory and spake with him concerning his decease which he should accomplish at Jerusalem. Now the prayer of Moses is fulfilled. He is called out of his grave to stand with Christ on Canaan's soil, the first-fruits, as it were, of them that shall be raised from the dead by the power of Christ's death and resurrection. That was a far grander destiny than to have led the hosts over the river Jordan in person. Moses may have been silent in his writings on the subject of immortality; but he is not silent in his life, for his appearance on the Mount to talk with Christ concerning his decease and atonement at Jerusalem demonstrates that God is not the God of the dead, but of the living.

So far as time was concerned, so far as this world was concerned, the great life of Moses ended in what strikes us as an overwhelming disappointment. But in the ages to come we see the prayer of Moses answered when he stands with Christ on the Mount. We all pass through disappointments, and they may become all the greater as life goes on, or as it approaches the end. But always these disappointments have in them the possibility of something greater.

All things are working together for good to you who love God.

> "O lonely grave in Moab's land!
>   O dark Beth-Peor's hill!
> Speak to these curious hearts of ours,
>   And teach them to be still.
> God hath His mysteries of grace,
>   Ways that we cannot tell;
> He hides them deep, like the hidden sleep
>   Of him he loved so well." [3]

[3] *Op. cit.*

XV. *Balaam—The man who reached for two worlds and lost both*

A BATTLEFIELD is
not a pleasant place for a walk; at least, not for half
a century or so after the battle has been fought. But
let us walk over this battlefield in Moab, across the
Jordan, where the children of Israel took vengeance
on the Midianites who had tempted them into licentiousness and sin. Here the slain lie in heaps, rows,
piles, and avenues, hecatombs of the dead. Already
the vultures and the jackals have come to the feast,
for where the carcass is, there also will the eagles be
gathered together. But who is this lying dead here
in this pyramid of fallen tribesmen and Bedouin, this
man with the robes of divination all rent and torn, his
gray hair clotted with blood, and his wild and sight-
less eyes staring heavenward? Balaam, is it thou?
Art thou also among the slain? How camest *thou*
here, Balaam? Art thou not he who once uttered
those great and eloquent words concerning the children of Israel and their destiny? Art thou not the

[196]

man who said, "God is not a man that he should lie,
nor the Son of man that he should repent"? Art
thou not he who said, "A star shall come out of
Jacob, and a scepter shall rise out of Israel"? Art
thou not he who made the prayer, "Let me die the
death of the righteous, and let my last end be like
his"? And yet, here thou liest—dead, slain among
the enemies of Israel! "And Balaam, son of Beor,
they slew with the sword."

When the children of Israel appeared on the borders of Moab and Midian, the kings of those countries, fearing that what had happened to Og, king of
Bashan, and Sihon, king of the Amorites, would happen to them, resolved to enlist in their services the
prophet and seer, Balaam, who lived far down on the
borders of the Euphrates. His reputation was that
whomsoever he cursed was cursed, and whomsoever
he blessed was blessed. When we have difficulties,
we sometimes think that the easier way is to push
them off on someone else, instead of facing them ourselves. So these two kings, instead of standing up
and fighting like men, if they thought Israel a dangerous invader, follow the plan of hiring Balaam to
curse them.

When Balaam received the ambassadors who had
come with the rewards of divination, asking Balaam
to curse Israel, the seer invited them to spend the
night at his home when he would inquire of the Lord.
In the night the message came to Balaam. "Thou

shalt not go with them. Thou shalt not curse the people, for they are blessed." At morning, Balaam reported this answer, and said to the ambassadors, "Get you into your land." When Balak, the king of Moab, received the prophet's refusal, evidently going on the ground that every man has his price, he sent yet again princes more and more honorable. They returned to Balaam and again asked him to come and curse Israel, telling him that Balak would promote him to very great honor.

This time Balaam, with a note of boasting which does not augur well for the future—for then as now, let not him that buckleth on his harness boast himself as he that layeth it aside—said to the embassy, "If Balak would give me his house full of silver and gold, I cannot go beyond the word of the Lord my God to do less or more." But then followed this dangerous invitation: "I pray you, tarry you also here this night that I may know what the Lord may say unto me more." Balaam is anxious to go and get the gold of Moab, if only he can secure the Lord's consent. In the night, Balaam seems to get the consent of the Lord, and early in the morning he saddled his ass and set off with the prince of Moab. But God's anger was kindled against him because he went.

On the journey the ass of Balaam turned out of the way into a path between two walls at a vineyard. Something had frightened the beast, and in trying a second time to get away, she crushed the prophet's foot against the wall, whereupon Balaam took to beating the ass. Then the cause of the animal's fright was disclosed to him, and he saw the angel of the Lord standing with a drawn sword in the path. When Balaam saw the angel with the sword, he was frightened and said, "I have sinned, for I knew not that thou stoodest in the way against me. Now, therefore, if it displease thee I will get me back again." But the angel of the Lord said, "Go with the men."

When he reached the borders of Moab, where Israel lay encamped, Balaam had the king of Moab build seven altars, from which the spirals of smoke went up to heaven. Then bidding Balak stand by the altars, Balaam went up to the top of a mountain to learn what God would have him say. As he surveyed the far-flung camp of Israel with the ark in the center and the standards of each tribe floating over them, what God said was this: "Who can count the dust of Jacob, and number the fourth part of Israel? Let me die the death of the righteous, and let my last end be like his." Disappointed, Balak took him to the top of Pisgah, and there again built seven altars. From Pisgah, Balak thought that Balaam would see only a small part of the camp of Israel. But again he was disappointed, for Balaam thus delivered himself. "Behold the people shall rise up as a great lion and lift up himself as a young lion." This time the angry Balak told Balaam neither to curse nor to bless. Still, he was hopeful of something better and brought him to the top of a third mountain, Peor. Again Balaam took his stand, and falling into a trance declared, "How goodly are thy tents, O Jacob, and thy tabernacles, O Israel. I shall see him, but not now; I shall behold him, but not nigh. There shall come a star out of Jacob, and a scepter shall rise out of Israel."

Disgusted at the outcome of his plan to have Israel cursed, Balak dismissed Balaam without gold or honor, and sent him back to his own country. But evidently the kings of Moab and Midian had some further dealings with Balaam, for it was at Balaam's suggestion that the children of Israel were brought into contact with the corrupt and idolatrous women of Moab and Midian. Thus, although he could not openly curse Israel, the crafty Balaam showed the kings of Moab and Midian how Israel could be made to curse itself. A fearful judgment fell upon the people because of their sin. This judgment over, the nation was summoned to make war on Midian, and avenge the dishonor done to the nation. In the battle which followed Midian was smitten and routed, and among the dead, for he had fought in the ranks of Midian, was the eloquent old prophet Balaam. "Balaam, son of Beor, they slew with the sword."

At first sight we might conclude that there is nothing in the history of this strange and enigmatical soothsayer which touches upon our life and thought today. But the more you look at him and study him, the more modern the prophet of the Euphrates appears. He is a timeless type of a man who tries to serve God and Mammon, who reaches for two worlds, the earthly and the heavenly, and loses both of them.

I. The Danger of Tampering and Trifling with Conscience

When the messengers of Balak came the first time, the will of God was plainly revealed, and without hesitation Balaam said he could not go, for he would not curse whom God had blessed. But on the second visit things are a little different. When the request is repeated, assuming an air of injured dignity, Balaam exclaimed, "If Balak would give me his house full of gold, I cannot go beyond the word of the Lord." But the effect of that high-sounding refusal is at once neutralized by the invitation which followed, asking these men to spend the night, and he would inquire again of the Lord. The Lord had made it perfectly plain what his will was; and yet Balaam is going to try to get the Lord to change his mind. He wants to get the gold of Moab and please himself, and yet, if possible, do so with the Lord's permission. This is the first step in the breakdown of Balaam's character. He shows how a man will lie, shift, shuffle, deceive others, and most of all himself, for the sake of his desires. His conscience spoke clearly when the first request was made. But Balaam did not obey, and begins to tamper and tease and coax his conscience until he thinks that he has got the consent of God. The Lord said, "Go with the men." But when Balaam went, the Lord was angry. Is there any inconsistency or contradiction there? No. God has said that with the upright he will show himself upright, and with the froward man he will show himself froward. Balaam was not true to the light that was in him, and this light became darkness in which he stumbled, having persuaded himself and deceived himself into thinking that God was with him. When we are not true to conscience, to the light which we have, we invite the darkness. That is what Christ meant when he said, "If thine eye be single, thy whole body shall be full of light. But if thine eye be evil, thy whole body shall be full of darkness. If therefore the light that is in thee be darkness, how great is that darkness."

General Grant, speaking of his chief of staff, says that Rawlins was a man who knew how to say No so emphatically to a request which he thought should not be granted, that the person he was addressing would understand at once there was no use of pressing the matter. The best defense against temptation is to have one courageous, single, decisive, ringing, and final No. What would you think of a ship's captain who, when sailing off a dangerous coast, saw suddenly through the clouds and the mist the flash of a lighthouse, and instead of at once altering his course,

MAN WHO REACHED FOR TWO WORLDS AND LOST BOTH

decided to go on a little further and wait for a second or third flash? He would be guilty, we say, of criminal folly and carelessness. Yet as the captains and masters of our souls, we often act as foolishly as the captain of that ship. Do not tamper with your conscience. Do not lightly dismiss the distinction which it makes between good and evil as only an inherited prejudice. Muffle not that bell. If it kept you awake last night, thank God that if you did sin, at least your conscience condemned you for it and the Spirit has not departed from you.

> "Then keep thy conscience sensitive,
>   No inward token miss;
> And go where grace entices thee.
>   Perfection lies in this."

II. No Man Goes to Judgment and Doom Un-
warned or without Obstacles Being
Placed in His Path

It was a sad day for Balaam as he sat dreaming beneath his palm trees on the far-off Euphrates when the ambassadors of Balak with the rewards of divination made their appearance and asked him to curse Israel. But God's hand was raised in warning at the very beginning, and from the day he received the invitation until that fatal day when he lay dead and dishonored among the Midianites, Balaam was repeatedly warned and went to his doom over a series and successions of obstacles, judgments, and warnings. God lets no one go away from him without warnings and without putting restraining obstacles in his way. In the case of Balaam, there was the plain word of God, the speech of the ass, the crushed foot, the sword of the angel, and yet over it all, Balaam rode roughshod to a dishonored grave.

Is anyone turning today from the true path? Has anyone been inclining toward sin? Is it altogether a primrose path? Or, even already, is there some hardship, some secret misgiving? Are there not things which are of a nature to make you think twice, to check and arrest you on the downward course— the appealing look in the eye of a friend, or the grief stamped on the face of a trusted wife or parent, or your own secret misgivings? In spite of all this, will you ride on to your doom?

When Balaam was frightened at the apparition of the angel with the sword, he said, but without real repentence, "I have sinned. I will go back." But the angel of the Lord sternly commanded him, "Go on with the men." When the swords of judgment began to flash, and things appear difficult and dangerous, men say they will turn and go back. But often, as in the case of Balaam, they cannot go back even if they want to. They have gone too far. They have let the current bear them too far down the river to turn now and stem it. The accumulation of habit, the repeated indulgence of desire, the repeated disobedience of God's word—all this says to them, like the angel of judgment whose sword flashed before the face of the frightened prophet on the way to Moab, "Go on! You cannot go back now."

III. The Insufficiency and Vanity of Religious Feelings and High Emotions without Religious Purpose, Obedience, and Deeds

Here is a man who had given him divine knowledge and illumination. So much so, that although he was one who stood without the circle of Israel's inspired prophets, he was the author of grand scriptural truth and prophetic forecast, such as hardly any prophet of the Old Testament was permitted to declare. Any anthology of the most beautiful and eloquent passages of the Bible would take in the eloquent and majestic utterances of the apostate prophet. "Let me die the death of the righteous," he cried, "and let my last end be like his." Yet how did he die? Alas, how did he die!

Do you like to sing the hymns? Does the federated worship of the church thrill you? Does your mind kindle with the great ideas of revelation and redemption, and even in your worst moments and after your worst deeds, do you feel that you would like to be a godly man and share in the godly man's eternal reward? Well and good; but you may be all that and feel all that in complete sincerity, and yet make as sad a shipwreck of it as did Balaam.

Religion demands a price. The trouble is that

people want the hopes and joys and rewards of religion without paying the price, just as Balaam wanted the destiny of God's people, which from his mountain altars he saw to be so glorious, without giving up the gold of Moab which had been promised him if he would only curse the people. In *Pilgrim's Progress* the Interpreter conducted Christian to where he beheld a stately palace on the top of which certain persons were walking who were clothed all in gold. Around the door stood a great company of men desirous to go in, but who dared not. A little distance from the door, at a table side, sat a man with a book and an ink horn to take the name of him that would enter into the palace. In the doorway stood many men in armor to keep it, being resolved to do what hurt and mischief they could to anyone who tried to enter. All were starting back in fear, and Christian himself was in a maze, when he saw a man of stout countenance go up to him with the ink horn and say, "Set down my name, sir!" The which when he had done, he saw the man draw his sword and put an helmet upon his head and rush toward the door upon the armed men, and after receiving and giving many wounds, he cut his way into the palace, and voices were heard of those who walked in gold raiment on the top of the palace, saying,

"Come in, come in,
Eternal Glory, thou shalt win."

It is not enough merely to wish to go in. It is not enough to have the man with the ink horn set your name down as an applicant. You must fight your way through. Balaam asked that his name be set down. "Let me die the death of the righteous, and let my last end be like his." But what was his end? "Balaam, son of Beor, they slew with the sword." He that persevereth to the end, the same shall be saved.

XVI. *Jonathan—The greatest friend in the Old Testament*

A FRIEND, when true, is one of life's greatest blessings; when false, one of life's sharpest thorns. David had a bitter experience with a false friend, and more than once he refers to that thorn in his spirit. "Mine own familiar friend," he says, "in whom I trusted, lifted up his heel against me." Had it been an enemy that reproached him, he said, he could have borne it. "But it was thou, a man mine equal, my guide and mine acquaintance. We took sweet counsel together, and walked into the house of God in company."

But this morning we deal with another kind of friend. It is a friend who never inspired David to write words like that, but a friend who inspired him to utter the noblest tribute in words ever paid to a friend. When the Amalekite who had fled from the battle on Mount Gilboa told David that Saul and Jonathan were dead, David poured out his soul in a touching and beautiful lament. In that lament are these words: "I am distressed for thee, my brother Jonathan. Very pleasant hast thou been unto me. Thy love to me was wonderful, passing the love of women." When Keats died, Shelley built him a great monument in his celebrated "Ode on the Death of John Keats." On the stone of Keats' grave beneath the cedars in a corner of the Protestant Cemetery at Rome are these fine lines by Severn:

> "Keats! if thy cherished name be 'writ in water,'
> Each drop has fallen from some mourner's cheek,
> A sacred tribute, such as heroes seek,
> Though oft in vain for dazzling deeds of slaughter.
> Sleep on: not honoured less for epitaph so meek."

Others have commemorated their friends in beautiful buildings and memorials. But this ode of David over Jonathan outranks them all. "Thy love to me was wonderful, passing the love of women." David had a great heart; a heart, if we may so say, whose strings were almost too open to the gentle, yet strong winds of affection, both of men and of women, But this was the great affection of David's life, his love for Jonathan. However one might question the title I have given to the previous sermons in this series on the heroes of the Old Testament, no one will question that to Jonathan belongs the title I have given him, "The Greatest Friend in the Old Testament," and, we might add, in the New; or in any of the Testaments or histories of the long Bible of the human race.

It is not often that history presents to us side by side two such men as David and Jonathan, for each in his way is incomparable. Yet here they are side by side in the drama of David's life. They met first on the day of David's great triumph over the Philistine colossus, Goliath. My own feeling is that when Goliath came out day after day to challenge the army of Israel and insult its God, and none answered his challenge, Jonathan must have been absent, or, if present, was ready and anxious to answer the challenge and do battle with the huge giant, but was restrained by his father. I say this on the ground of the past record of Jonathan, for on two occasions he had appeared as Israel's hero and done valiant battle against the Philistines. His exploits at Geba and Michmash, where almost single-handed he had put the enemies of his country to flight, had made him the hero and favorite of the people; so much so that when Saul would have put him to death because he had unknowingly transgressed a commandment not to eat on the day of battle, the people rose up and told Saul that not a hair of his head should fall to the ground. Jonathan's high reputation for friendship sometimes hides from us the very important fact that he was also, up to the time of the advent of David, the nation's most popular hero.

When David, after slaying the giant, came to the headquarters of Saul, it was a case of love at first sight between him and Jonathan. The cheers of the people and the songs of the women were bitterness and gall to King Saul. He could not tolerate the thought that David was a hero with the people, and from that day and forward Saul eyed David with a fierce and insane jealousy. But with Jonathan it was different. He had more to lose by the popularity of David than Saul. He was the crown prince, the next to the throne, and, until that day, the most popular man in Israel. It was all to his advantage that David's heroic deed should be discounted and belittled. The ordinary man would have done that. He would have resented bitterly the cheers of the army and the songs of the women over David, for it meant the eclipse of his own popularity. But Jonathan from the very beginning is natural, or, we might almost say, supernatural, spontaneous, and wholly unselfish in his friendship. He forgets all about his own fame and his own prospects and lets his soul go out in love and admiration to the ruddy youth from the sheep folds. He forgot himself, and by so doing forgot himself into immortality.

Sometimes friendships have a selfish basis. Men talk of making "contacts," they join a club, or an association, for the sake of contacts, and acquaintances and friendships are formed on that basis. But here is the greatest friendship of history, a love at first sight and one that many waters could not quench nor floods of adversity drown; and yet on one side, on the side of Jonathan, the man who was the leader

in this friendship had nothing whatever to gain, but
from the standpoint of this world everything to lose.
The higher David rose the lower must sink the fortunes of Jonathan. If David became king, Jonathan
would lose the throne. On his side there was nothing
to gain; nothing but what perhaps was the greatest
of all, the fervent love of a great heart like David's.
That meant more to Jonathan than the cheers of the
army, the songs of the women, or the scepter of
Israel.

The sacrificial and disinterested nature of this
immortal friendship is related in what we are told
Jonathan did at this first meeting. He made a
covenant of friendship with David, because he loved
him as his own soul. The commandment is, "Thou
shalt love thy neighbor as thyself." Jonathan seems
to have been the only man who ever did it. There
is no doubt that he actually loved David as his own
soul. For what did he do? He stripped himself of
his robe and gave it to David; also, his garments and
his girdle; even his sword and his bow. This was the
way they sealed their covenant. When God made the
covenant with Noah he sealed it with the rainbow.
When he made the covenant with Abraham he sealed
it in blood. When a man makes a covenant with
woman in marriage he seals it with a ring. But when
Jonathan made his covenant with David he stripped
himself of all that he had and sealed it with his robe,
his sword, his girdle, and his bow. It was a covenant

that Jonathan never broke, and through all the ups and downs of his life David had that house of refuge, the love and friendship of Jonathan.

This, of course, was no merely human friendship. We miss the grandeur of it completely if we do not see that this temple of love stands upon a firm foundation of faith. Perhaps godly Samuel had been a tutor of Jonathan, and had taught him to have faith in God. It is clear from the beginning that Jonathan believes that the hand of God is upon David, and he is eager and ready to forward David toward the great goal which was in store for him.

This was a friendship that had much pain in it, for the course of true love never runs smooth. Jonathan has the pain of the difficult and trying situation in which he found himself, to love David as his friend, and yet be loyal to Saul, his king and father. He managed to maintain that loyalty, and also be true to his friend; although in doing so he jeopardizes his own life, for Saul threw his javelin not only at David, but at Jonathan. When David, after the last attack by Saul, is almost in despair and says to Jonathan, "There is but a step between my soul and death," Jonathan assures him that he shall not die, and arranges with David a device to test once more the feeling of Saul toward David. David is to absent himself on a given day from the royal table. If Saul takes it well, David will be apprized thereof and brought back to the court. But if he takes it ill,

Jonathan will warn his friend and help him to escape.
On the appointed day Saul at once noted the absence
of David, and said, "Wherefore cometh not the son
of Jesse to meat?" Dissatisfied and angry at Jonathan's answer, Saul hurled his javelin at his own son.
Then Jonathan went out into the field where David
was in hiding and sadly and reluctantly let him know
of the implacable mood of Saul. The plan was that
Jonathan was to pretend to be practicing in archery.
He was to shoot three arrows across the field near
the thicket where David was in hiding. If, after he
had shot, David heard him say to his armor bearer,
"The arrows are on this side of thee," David would
know that all was well. But if he shot beyond
David and said to the lad, "Is not the arrow beyond
thee?" David would know that his life was in danger.
With a heavy heart Jonathan took up his bow, fixed
the arrow, and then drove it far beyond the thicket
where David was hiding. David heard the twang of
the bow and the song of the arrow, and knew how
things stood, even before he heard Jonathan cry out
to his armor bearer, "Is not the arrow beyond thee?"
The armor bearer was sent back to the palace. David
came out of hiding, and the two men, recognizing the
sad fate in store for them, kissed one another and
wept in their sorrow. This time it was David who
"exceeded." Apparently, his sorrow on this occasion
was greater even than the sorrow of Jonathan. Both
hearts were heavy and sore; but the brave Jonathan

bids his friend depart and tells him that the Lord will be between them; that is, he will be with them both. The best of friendships ultimately must hear the twang of the bow which sounds the music of parting and separation. Yet, where there is faith, one can say to the other, "Go in peace; we have both sworn in the name of the Lord; we both believe in God, and in him there is no separation." "Though sundered far, by faith we meet around the common mercy seat."

This was a friendship which grew warmer and greater as the clouds of adversity grew heavier. It was no mere summer friendship. The ancient Greeks took for the symbol of true friendship a young man upon whose garments were written the words, "Summer and winter." Certainly we can discern those words written upon the garments of Jonathan. The greater the danger David was in, and the darker the day of his adversity, the brighter shines the friendship of Jonathan. In *Great Expectations*, when Pip came for the last time to see his benefactor, the ex-convict who had been condemned to be hanged, Magwich, taking the lad by the hand, said, "You have never deserted me, boy; and what's the best of all, you've been more comfortable alonger me since I was under a dark cloud than when the sun shone. That's the best of all." In the extraordinary experiences of the former king of the utilities enterprises in this country, Samuel Insull, there is at least one pleasing incident. Conversing on the deck of a ship that bore him back to the country whose jurisdiction he had fled, the ex-financier and promoter, explaining how he came to have funds to live on in his exile, said this, "When a man is down, the usual thing is that his friends desert him. But I have been surprised to discover that there were not a few friends who remembered me in my adversity and were glad to help me." If this is true, certainly everyone will be glad that it is true. Jonathan was the friend born for adversity, the brother who loveth at all times. He was like Paul's famous friend, the Ephesian Christian, Onesiphorus, who came to visit Paul in prison in Rome. Paul hands him down to immortality with this fine ecomium, "He was not ashamed of my chains." If you are a real friend to your friend, then you will not be ashamed of his chains.

The highest manifestation of Jonathan's friendship came in the darkest hour of David's life. He was a fugitive and an outlaw, weary with constant danger and flight, and beginning to lose his grip on himself, and, what is more, his faith in God. He is in hiding in the wood of Ziph, a tangle of trees and thickets in the mountainous country near Hebron, and his stronghold is surrounded by the soldiers of Saul. It was a dangerous time for David, perhaps the darkest hour of his life; and a dangerous time, too, for Jonathan to show his friendship for the hunted outlaw. But at midnight Jonathan arose and went to David and "strengthened his hand in the Lord." He told him that God had kept him in the past and would keep him in the future. He made him believe again in his destiny, telling him that he would be king, and that all he asked was that he, Jonathan, might be next to him, and that if they never met again in life, David would show the kindness of God to his family. The two friends renewed their covenant and parted, never to meet again in this world.

That was the great service that Jonathan did for David. He strengthened his hand in God. There are friendships which do not do that. On the contrary, they weaken one's hold on God. "He had a friend," is the sad epitaph which might well be written on the grave of thousands, and across the brow of thousands of others who, if not actually dead and in their graves, might better be there. Their friendship was the fountain of their sorrow and their woe. But that was not true of Jonathan. That is the test of the highest friendship, whether or not it strengthens your hand in God. If your friend is taking your hand out of the hand of God, then, no matter what the pain, no matter if it be like the tearing out of the flesh, renounce and forsake that friendship.

Whose hand can you strengthen in God? Whom do you know who is this night, this day, in the wood of Ziph, caught in the tangles of sorrow, or debt, or distress, or transgression, sin? Your letter, your word, your visit, your prayer, may be to him like that midnight visit of Jonathan to David in the wood of Ziph.

This friendship had a beautiful postlude, or, better, a golden afterglow. Jonathan has fallen in battle on Mount Gilboa. Now, years afterward, David has vanquished the house of Saul. All who can dispute his claim are dead, or disarmed, and David is seated securely on the throne of Israel. What is the first thing he does? What is the first thing he asks? For some supporter of the house of Saul upon whom he can take vengence for all the cruelties and hardships, to which Saul and his house had subjected him? No; David was never grander or more kingly, never more "a man after God's heart," than at that moment. What he said was this: "Is there yet any left of the house of Saul that I may show him kindness for Jonathan's sake?" When he learns that there is a poor lame son left, Mephibosheth, he sends for him and brings him to his family at the court. In the wood of Ziph Jonathan had asked him to be kind to his family, to show the kindness of God to them. David remembers that, and in the very language of Jonathan asks for any of his children that he may "show them the kindness of God."

The noble and beautiful life of Jonathan lets us know that even in this world with sin and sorrow and cruelty and treachery and difficulties and temptations all about us, a beautiful and Christlike character is a possibility. Forever Jonathan tells us what it is possible for us to be in life. Aim high; and you cannot aim higher than Jonathan.

All through this sermon you must have been thinking, I am sure, of another Friend, the Crown Prince of Heaven, the King's own and only Son, whose love to you is wonderful, passing even the love of Jonathan. In all that Jonathan was and did he is a type and a suggestion of the Friend of sinners. Jonathan made a covenant with David and sealed it with his garment and his sword and his bow. Christ comes to make a covenant with you, a lost sinner, and seals it with his precious blood. Jonathan stripped himself for David. Christ strips himself for you. He was rich, but for your sake he became poor; he had a throne in heaven, but for your sake he hung upon the cursed Cross. Jonathan gave David his robe. Christ gives you his robe, the robe of his forgiveness, the robe of his righteousness, a robe that has been made white in his precious blood. When you are lost and cut and bruised in the tangles of sin or pain or shame or sorrow, he comes at midnight to strengthen your hand in God. He says, "You believe in God, believe also in me."

Is this Friend of sinners your Friend? Have you made your covenant with him? If so, is there anything now in your life that is false to that Friend and that friendship? If he is not your Friend, if you cannot sing, "What a Friend we have in Jesus," then remember the hour will come when that Friend will be your greatest need. If you make him your Friend, he will never leave you nor forsake you. No matter what your mistakes or sins may be, or have been, still he calls you "friend." Even Judas, who betrayed him with a kiss, Jesus in the Garden of Gethsemane addressed as "friend." Even Peter, who cursed him and swore that he had never seen him— all that Jesus asked of Peter when they next met was this, "Lovest thou me?" His friendship will be the greatest and sweetest thing in this life; and in the life to come, when you join the blood-washed throng about his throne, then, in a nobler, sweeter song, you will be able to say, "Thy love unto me was wonderful."

XVII. *Nehemiah—The bravest man in the Old Testament*

MIDDAY, in the palace of the king of Persia at Shushan, where the yellow Ulai winds about the walls of the palace. Within the palace Artaxerxes, the long-handed despot of the world, with his queen at his side, is seated at the banqueting table, attended by obsequious slaves and hundreds of his nobles and satraps. The hall is worthy of the empire. White, blue, and green curtains drape the walls, caught with purple cords to silver rings fixed in pillars of marble. The pavement is of red, blue, white, and black marble, and the couches of gold. Clouds of incense go up, and the strains of music float through the halls.

Yet in this crowd of banqueters and courtiers there is one sad face and heavy heart. It is Nehemiah, who had come as a youth from Jerusalem with the Hebrew captives. He had risen by industry, character, and personal charm to a high office at the Persian court, and was now the cupbearer to Artaxerxes. The despot of the world, looking about him, noted the sad face of his handsome cupbearer and said to him, "Why is thy countenance sad, seeing thou art not sick? This is nothing else but sorrow of heart." The face is the infallible index of the soul, and when the heart is heavy or sad the face registers that sorrow in a way which cannot be mistaken. Artaxerxes was correct in his inference. The look on the face of Nehemiah was not the shadow caused by pain or sickness, but the shadow cast by sorrow. So rightly concluded the king, when he said, "This is nothing but sorrow of heart."

At first, alarmed at the king's question, Nehemiah answered, "O King, live forever!" Then he gave him the reason for his sorrow. Sometime before, taking the air at the eventide on the walls of the palace, Nehemiah had heard men speaking his own tongue. In a foreign land, after straining to catch the accent of a strange tongue, nothing sounds so good as a voice speaking your own language. Nehemiah turned to talk with these Hebrews, and asked them about the condition of the colony which had gone up thirty years before with Ezra. The answer he received filled him with sorrow. The Jews at Jerusalem were in a desperate plight, much worse than their compatriots who were in exile, and as for the city itself, the walls were broken down and its gates burned with fire. Nehemiah might have dismissed these tidings lightly, shrugged his shoulders, and said, "It's too bad; what an ending for the once glorious city of David and of Solomon! But I must not mourn over it. Persia now is my country. Here is my career and my destiny." But he was not that kind of a Jew. He was the kind of a Jew who liked to say, "If I forget thee, O Jerusalem, let my right hand forget her cunning. Let my tongue cleave to the roof of my mouth if I remember not thee above my chief joy."

These tidings smote the heart of the cupbearer as if the Jewish pilgrims had brought him the news of the death of a member of his family. "This," he said to the king, "is the reason for my sorrow. Why should not my countenance be sad, when the city, the place of my fathers' sepulchers, lieth waste, and the gates thereof are consumed with fire?" The compassionate king asked him what he would have and what he would choose. Nehemiah responded, "If it please the King, that thou wouldst send me unto Judah unto the city of my fathers' sepulchers, that I may build it." The king readily gave his consent, and with a small escort and letters which gave him the right to requisition labor and building material, Nehemiah set out on the fifteen-hundred-mile journey to Jerusalem.

Arrived there, after a three days' rest, Nehemiah, in the dead of the night, telling no man his design, went out by the gate of the valley before the dragon wall and rode around the walls of the city, noting where they were broken and crumbling and where the gates were fallen and burned with fire. The next day, knowing the worst as to the condition of the city, he summoned the leaders of the people, told them why he had come from the court of Persia, and appealing to their religion and their patriotism, asked them to join him in rebuilding the walls of the city. The response was enthusiastic and universal. All classes of people, the rich and the poor, the peasants and the nobles, commenced the work of restoration. Fifteen hundred miles away, the task of rebuilding Jerusalem may not have seemed so formidable. But viewed close at hand, it was a different matter. Yet the desolation of the walls and the great difficulty of the restoration did not discourage Nehemiah. His vision fifteen hundred miles away sustained him now when he was face to face with reality.

The work, however, started with such enthusiasm and zeal, at once encountered serious obstacles and hindrances. The leaders of the mixed and hybrid Jews, the Samaritans, Sanballat and Tobiah, and their Arabian ally, Geshem, unwilling to have Jerusalem restored to power and influence, took every means to prevent Nehemiah from carrying out his project. They first tried the plan of ridicule and mockery. Coming to the walls where the Jews were working they said, "What do these feeble Jews? Will they fortify themselves? Do they think they can revive the stones out of the heaps of the rubbish which are burned? What kind of a wall is this? Why, if even a fox, prowling by night should step on their wall, it would break down under him." But Nehemiah and his men went on with their work. "So we built the wall," is the refrain which runs all through this chorus of the hammer, the trowel, and the sword.

Then Sanballat and his confederates, gathering their tribesmen, planned to stop the building operations by force of arms. Nehemiah answered by arming all his workmen. Half of the men toiled on the walls, while the other half held the spear, the shield, and the bow. By the side of Nehemiah there was always the trumpeter, ready to sound the alarm. The Samaritans had no taste for an actual conflict, and changing their tactics when they have been foiled, tried to tempt Nehemiah to come down from the walls and have a consultation with them, with the suggestion of some sort of a compromise. "Come, now," they said, "and let us reason together." But Nehemiah answered, "I am doing a great work and I cannot come down." Then, as is usual, the enemies of truth resorted to their favorite weapon, slander. False letters were written and taken into the city by a prophet who had been bribed. In these letters it was alleged that there were rumors that Nehemiah was fomenting a rebellion, and was planning to make himself an independent king. Even the breath of such a charge was enough to take the head off a man's shoulders. The false prophet who brought this letter said to Nehemiah, "This is serious business. If I were you, I would go into the temple and take sanctuary there. Lay hold on the horns of the altar, and the avenger's sword cannot harm you." But Nehemiah, never more magnificent than at this moment, answered, "Should such a man as I flee? Should such a man as I go into the temple to save his life? I will not go in."

Thus, undeceived by craft and guile, unmoved by ridicule, unintimidated by threats and unfrightened by slander, Nehemiah finished his great work. "So the wall was finished." When the work had been completed, to the accompaniment of music, shouts of rejoicing, and the reading of the law by Ezra, the wall was dedicated to the glory of God and the prosperity of Israel. When the sun rose out of the east beyond the mountains of Moab, the finished towers and turrets of the city's wall reflected its golden light.

The Church always stands in need of a man like Nehemiah. Every government and every city sorely needs a man of his caliber. But this morning I take Jerusalem as the type and symbol of that sacred city which is within us all. The walls of our city, our holy place, the soul, are built on the lines of their grand and original design, when God made man in his image, even though these walls and gates are now broken and wasted. To every man there comes the moment when he feels the call to rebuild and strengthen the walls of his heart, and, as in the case of Nehemiah and Jerusalem, the builder will be confronted by enemies from within and enemies without.

Man is like one of the old Greek temples, whose
ruins, like that of Neptune at Sunium, arouse our
interest and admiration and make us wonder what the
perfect temple must have been. Although the roof,
the walls, the pillars are fallen, and the stones covered
with rubbish and earth, yet one can trace the outlines
of the temple and see where the walls went up and
where the mighty columns, so exquisitely carved, cast
their long shadows. It matters not what has happened to man, the foundation of his greatness is
clearly to be discerned. I can never give up the
Christian and biblical idea of man. The growing
brute theory fits not nearly so well the facts of human nature as the Bible theory of a great city, fallen
and desolate, but still capable of restoration and redemption. I am still ready to say with Robert South,
that Aristotle was but the wreck of an Adam, and
Athens but the rubbish of an Eden.

As Nehemiah in his far-off exile got the word about
the condition of the holy city, which produced sorrow and repentance, and gave birth to the ambition
to rebuild the walls, so conscience brings to man at
some hours disturbing tidings about himself. He is
compelled to ask himself, "Is it well with my soul?"
and if he is honest with himself, he must answer that
here and there it is not altogether well. This gate
is fallen; the wall is undermined, weakened, or broken
down.

At such a time there is born a sincere desire and

purpose, a reformation and improvement. We think of what we might be, and ought to be, and say within our hearts that what we ought to be, and can be, we will be.

> "O for a man to rise in me,
> That the man I am might cease to be."

There is nothing unusual and nothing strange about this awakening of knowledge concerning ourselves, the conviction that things ought to be different and better, and the purpose to make them so. But, alas, some go on further than the vision and its purpose. The thing seems so difficult that they do not even start. Others set forth, but the difficulties in the way cool their ardor, and sinking back into the old ways, they acquiesce in their ignoble selves.

The work of rebuilding the walls of the city of our soul involves, first of all, self-denial. Moses had to choose between a life of distinction and ease as the son of Pharaoh's daughter and the leadership of God's people in the wilderness. But he made his choice and esteemed the reproach of Christ greater riches than the treasures of Egypt. The Persian despot said to Nehemiah, Choose! Choose between the high office and easy life of the king's cupbearer, and the fifteen-hundred-mile journey with its difficult and discouraging task of rebuilding at the end. But Nehemiah chose, and he chose for his soul, not for his body. There will be difficulties in the way, and self-denial will be required when a man chooses for his soul. But the price paid will be supremely worth while.

To carry out the high purpose of soul rebuilding requires, once more, meditation, introspection, and solitude. It was when he went apart by himself and was on his knees that the great purpose was born in Nehemiah's mind and heart, and it was during his solitary midnight ride around the walls of the city that he outlined his plan and resolved upon the undertaking. The world today doesn't give men much chance for meditation, introspection, or going apart. The world is ever with us, in one form or another. Today, men, when they get up in the morning, hear the voice of the world, and that voice, whether in music, advertisement, description, or in the tones of the prophets of the radio who have eclipsed in fame the minor prophets, is ever sounding in their ears. There are still multitudes of lonely people in the world, but never a time when men were so little alone. Those who do not "at least checker their lives with solitude will never unfold the capacities which are in them." "Be still and know that I am God." So we can say also to ourselves, "Be still and know that thou art not a sounding board, nor a clothes horse, nor an endless chain of activity, but a living soul."

To rebuild the walls of the soul will require courage. It will take courage to resist the invitation and the temptation to compromise and to lower our ideals. We live in a world where there are so many people with whom we must come in contact who have compromised their principles, surrendered them altogether, or who never had any to begin with. And such a world is ever pressing close upon man and seeking to mold him into conformity. The answer of the soul ought to be that of the fearless wall builder of Jerusalem, "I am doing a great work, and I cannot come down. Come up here, if you will, and if you can pay the price; but I will not go down."

This work will require the courage again to face ridicule. To differ from people, to do, not as the majority do, but to do what you ought to do, to stand by your principles, whether many, or one, with none to stand by your side, takes the courage to ignore that polished shaft of Satan, mockery and ridicule. Nehemiah, when they told him his wall was such a poor job that even a fox's paw would break it through, went quietly on with his business. David, when his brothers laughed at him, and wanted to know what he had done with the few sheep in the wilderness, went on with his business and selected his five smooth stones out of the brook, and in every stone saw reflected the head of his fallen and colossal adversary. Far better to let others laugh at you than to be compelled to laugh at yourself, or have God laugh at you.

To be faithful to the soul and this great work of

rebuilding its wall invites, as was the case of this ancient builder, slander and vilification. Then comes the supreme test, whether or not a man can stand that test. Will he be frightened from his duty when some-one impugns his motives, questions his sincerity, or hurls at him that favorite brick and missile of little minds, "hypocrite"? Or, will he take his stand and say with Nehemiah, "Should such a man as I flee?"

Here, we can never say of the walls of the city of our soul what Nehemiah said of the walls of Jerusa-lem, "So we finished the wall." Always, because of the ceaseless opposition of the corruption of our hearts and the wear and tear of this world, there is one or another part of our wall that needs strengthen-ing and reinforcement, and gates which must be set up again. Nevertheless, we look forward to the day when these walls, restored and unbroken, shall be dedicated again to the glory of God, and when the rising sun of immortality shall smite the towers and turrets of the finished wall, and we shall all come unto a perfect man. unto the measure of the stature of a perfect man in Christ.

XVIII. *David—The greatest sinner and the greatest saint in the Old Testament*

FOR David's sake! That is God's estimate of David. Solomon, who started so well, had become an apostate, going after strange women and building temples for the heathen gods. Judgment is to fall upon him and his kingdom, but for the sake of David his father, this judgment will not take place in the days of Solomon. What a beautiful and touching tribute to David's memory! God knew the tenderness of David's heart, and only because Solomon is his son, the judgment which is to fall upon the nation will be postponed.

After I have seen the face of my Lord, and after those faces which I have loved and lost awhile, and perhaps after St. Paul also, the one I would like to see first in heaven is David. Some things stand out above others in one's recollection of the past. One of these unerasable memories is the reading of the eleventh chapter of II Samuel at family worship. I can see the fires burning on the hearth, and the family assembled for morning worship; and I remember very distinctly the solemn words with which the reading of this chapter was prefaced.

It would not do for such a chapter to be read out of any other book. The Bible alone can relate such things and leave the reader elevated in mind and purified in life. When we read this terrible chapter with its narrative of David's sin, we are tempted to wish that David had died before his life wrote this awful chapter. But God knows best. If David had died before this incident, the Bible would have been lacking the account of what is, in some respects, the greatest sin and the greatest repentance. St. Augustine, in commencing his *Commentary on the Fifty-First Psalm*, says: "With grief indeed we speak, and with trembling. But yet God would not have to be hushed what he hath willed to be written."

Alexander of Macedon used to be painted with his hand resting on his face, as if in reverie. But the real purpose was to hide the scar on his cheek. The Bible paints men just as they are; no scar, birthmark, or deformity, however odious and hideous, is left out. All theories as to human nature vanish and disappear before the fact. To know what man is, all one needs to do is to read what man has done.

> "Not in their brightness, but their earthly stains,
> Are the true seed vouchsafed to earthly eyes.
> And saints are lowered that the world may rise."

In that powerful and fascinating piece of literature, *Mark Rutherford's Deliverance,* the sequel to *Mark Rutherford's Autobiography,* Mark Rutherford describes a Sunday morning visit which he and his friend McKay made to a freethinking hall in London, where they listened to a debate between an evangelical minister and an agnostic. When the minister had finished with an earnest plea for his hearers to repent and believe on Christ, he was followed by his freethinking antagonist. The minister had spoken of the life to come and of the bliss which awaited redeemed men in the eternal companionship of the Most High and with the spirits of just men made perfect. His adversary commenced by discounting such an inducement, declaring that although the New Cut, a miserable section of London, was a poor sort of place, he would rather sit there all day with his feet on a basket than lie in the bosom of some of the just men made perfect portrayed in the Bible. David, above all the others, he singled out as the most notorious of these eminent saints, and, amid the uproarious applause of his auditors, he rehearsed his crimes and declared that this "treacherous villain" would have been tried by a jury of twelve men and hung outside Newgate if he had lived in the nineteenth century.

The freethinker's sneer, one of the stock arguments on the part of those who wish that Christianity were not true, was an echo or a fulfilment of the prophet

Nathan's words, who, when he convicted David of his transgression, pronounced the severest judgments upon David's family, "because by this deed thou hast given great occasion to the enemies of the Lord to blaspheme." No sin that was ever sinned has given such occasion to the enemies of the Lord to blaspheme as the sin of David.

I. DAVID'S SIN AND CRIME

While to us this sin is shocking and in itself, and by reason of several aggravations, is heinous, we ought not to forget that in David's age it was not so regarded. David was an absolute monarch, and as such could take into his harem whom he pleased and kill whom he desired. The thing to note here is that, although this was so, David was greatly troubled about his crime and took extraordinary means to cover it up and to save himself from punishment.

Probably this was no sudden breakdown in David's character, but, as is almost always the case, the last step in a long decline toward evil. We doubt not that his communion with God, about which he could sing so sweetly, had been interrupted before the time and occasion of his fall. The sin of David shows, as few chapters in the book of human wickedness and depravity do, the way in which one sin suggests, and sometimes demands, another. First, the idle hour upon the roof of his palace, when he ought to have been at the head of his army at the siege of Rabbah.

If what David saw he had at once put out of his mind, he might have been saved. We are not responsible for temptations coming to our door; but we are responsible for entertaining them. As Luther put it, "I can't keep the birds from flying over my head, but I can keep them from building their nests under my hat."

The worst part of David's sin is not in connection with Bathsheba, but in connection with her husband, the loyal and upright Uriah. Here the man after God's heart appears as a subtle and malignant demon, like the price of perdition himself. His first thought, because his conscience troubles him and fears startle him, is to save himself from exposure and from vengeance. When the frank and upright Uriah, through his very affection and loyalty to the king, cannot be entrapped into the king's plot, then David plans for his death, not by his own hand, but by the hand of the enemy in battle. He told the captain of the host, Joab, to set Uriah in the forefront of the hottest battle, and then in the midst of the fight retire from him that he might be smitten and die. Thus he would be got out of the way, and apparently would have died a hero's death. Joab carried out the plan and Uriah fell in battle. The crafty Joab charged the messenger who carried word of Uriah's death to David to tell the king, if he seemed to be angry that so rash an assault was made on Rabbah, "Thy servant Uriah the Hittite is dead also." When the messenger of Joab had told of the repulse and the death of many of David's soldiers, and then concluded by saying, "And Uriah the Hittite died also," David, as if to comfort Joab, and at the same time pay a tribute to Uriah, sent this message to Joab, who, being in the plot, must have smiled when he read it: "Let not this thing displease thee, for the sword devoureth one as well as another. Make thy battle more strong against the city, and overthrow thou it." When a decent period of mourning was over, David married Bathsheba. "But"—and the narration of this crime and sin must always be read in the light of this sentence—"but the thing that David had done, displeased the Lord."

During this period between the time of the consummation of his crime and the coming of the prophet to denounce him, we are not to think of David as altogether happy, and totally indifferent to his sin. It is true, indeed, that sin has terrible powers of deception, and that nothing so blinds us to our sin as the very fact that it is ours. Nevertheless, I cannot believe that David, in view of his past history, in view of his native generosity and tenderness, and in view of the God-ward outlook of his life, was altogether without the piercings of conscience. There must have been days when, seated on his roof garden, where he had the vision which led him on to his sin and crime of adultery and murder, he wished that his eyes had been blinded before he had lapsed, and perhaps he would have been willing to give all his kingdom for the peace of mind he had before he fell. But regret is not repentance. The fall and sack of Rabbah, related in a previous chapter, probably belongs to the period between the murder of Uriah and the coming of Nathan. If so, the terrible, barbarous, and for him, unusual, punishment which he meted out to the captured people of Rabbah can be understood. Sometimes, when all is not right within, these external cruelties and ferocities are the expression of a troubled soul. David was "stumbling upon the dark mountains."

II. The Coming of Nathan

However David suffered, he did not repent. "Then the Lord sent Nathan unto David." The minister's most difficult mission is not to break the news of death to some wife, or child, but to do what Nathan did on this occasion, to speak with one about his sin. Never did a man have a more difficult sermon to preach. David was not only Nathan's king, but his friend. Together they had planned for the building of the temple, and for the order of its service. Together they had walked unto the house of God and taken sweet counsel; and, no doubt, Nathan had oft been charmed with David's music and conversation. Now he must go to rebuke him for his sin. Yet happy was David, who had a Nathan to come to him, and happy is every man to whom some God-sent Nathan comes with the message of God.

Never was a more tender and yet more severe sermon preached by mortal lips. The plan of Nathan is to have David pass sentence upon an imaginary case, and then show him that he has denounced himself. What a parable this is, Nathan's parable of the lost Lamb! Worthy to stand side by side with that other parable of the Lost Sheep by David's greater Son.

When he came to the palace with his heavy heart, Nathan said: "There were two men in one city; the one rich and the other poor. The rich man had exceeding many flocks and herds; but the poor man had nothing, save one little ewe lamb, which he had bought and nourished up. And it grew up together with him and with his children. It did eat of his own meat, and drink of his own cup, and lay in his bosom, and was unto him as a daughter." What a picture that is of domestic happiness and a household pet! One can almost see the little lamb playing with the children, drinking out of their cup at the table, and sleeping on their bed. "And there came a traveler unto the rich man, and he spared to take of his own flock and of his own herd, to dress for the wayfaring man that was come unto him, but took the poor man's lamb and dressed it for the man that was come to him."

Even hearing the faint echo of this parable, as we read it in the Old Testament, serves to rouse our indignation against such a monster of heartlessness, selfishness, and injustice; and we all feel like saying what David said, "As the Lord liveth, the man that hath done this thing shall surely die; and he shall restore the lamb fourfold because he did this thing, and because he had no pity." The thing to which Nathan makes his appeal is David's sense of justice and pity, and the thing which he stresses in the conduct of the rich man is his heartlessness and selfishness. After all, every kind of sin can be defined in the terms of selfishness. There is the root of all evil; and so we understand what was meant when the summary of the Ten Commandments was given in these words, "Thou shalt love the Lord thy God, and thy neighbor as thyself."

"As the Lord liveth," cried David, reaching for his sword, "the man that hath done this thing shall surely die!" The words were no more than out of his mouth when Nathan said, "Thou art the man!" How could David have missed the point of this exquisite but powerful parable! Only because sin has this strange power to blind us to its presence. All sins look odious save our own, until conscience is awakened. "Thou art the man!" said Nathan. "You were king of Israel, and possessed riches and comforts, palaces and servants, wives, slaves, and concubines. But not satisfied with that for your base indulgence, you had to take the only wife of Uriah, the Hittite, your faithful friend and soldier. And not only did you take his wife, but you took his life. You were not man enough to do it with your own sword, but had him slain in the battle with the sword of the children of Ammon."

III. David's Repentance

Now David saw what Nathan meant. He saw himself like the rich man, a monster of heartlessness and cruelty, and exlaimed, "I have sinned against the Lord!" There is no resentment against Nathan, no foolish effort to exculpate himself, as Saul did when he said, "I have sinned"; no brazen denial of his transgression; but simple and sincere and unreserved confession; "I have sinned against the Lord." If it had been any other oriental monarch to whom Nathan had come with such a message, he would have had his head cut off for his pains; but David said, "I have sinned." Then Nathan said, "The Lord hath put away thy sin." Before we speak of that wonderful forgiveness, let us pause for a moment to consider the punishment which came upon David even though he was forgiven.

The temporal penalties upon sin were not remitted. Nathan pronounces the judgment upon the guilty but now penitent king. This judgment is to consist of the following terrible elements: First, the sword shall never depart from David's house. With the sword he had slain the faithful Uriah. Now the sword would ever flash in his own house, and in his own kingdom. Second, because of his wickedness evil would be raised up against him out of his own house. Third, as he had violated and profaned another man's home, so he would live to see his own home desecrated and his own wives ravished. Fourth, the child which had been born, and which, although it had lived but a brief time, had lived long enough to twine the tendrils of affection about the father's heart, would die. Fifth, David had done his wickedness secretly. The retribution would be public, in the sight of the whole nation.

The particular reason given for these terrible and public punishments is that David's sin has made the enemies of God to blaspheme. In every age that has been so.

How often has the sneer been repeated, and how often has it been said that David confessed his sin and repented only when he could no longer hide it and when judgment threatened him. The answer to all this is to read the list of punishments which fell upon David, and the series of agonies through which he passed. He had to bear not only his own grief for the child, but the anguish of its mother. "He that doeth wrong," says St. Paul, "shall receive the wrong which he hath done." In other words, not only are we punished for our sins, but very often the punishment assumes the form of the sin which we have committed. Jacob deceived Esau, and lived to be cruelly deceived by his own sons. David defiled another man's home, and lived to see his own home defiled. He befouled himself with sensuality and animalism, and lived to see his own daughter defiled by Amnon. He was a traitor to his faithful soldier, Uriah, and lived to see his own army turn against him. He slew Uriah with the sword, and lived to see the sword in the hand of Absalom murder his brother Amnon and flash in the rebellion led by the king's beloved son. That David recognized retributive justice in these woes which came upon him, is shown, first of all, by what he said when Shimei cursed him when David had to flee the city. One of the king's followers wanted to cut off the head of Shimei; but David said, "Let him alone, and let him curse; for the Lord hath bidden him." And second, by the words of David's lament when the runner from the battle in the wood of Ephraim delivered his terrible tidings, and said in answer to David's inquiry, "Is the young man Absalom safe?" "The enemies of my lord the king, and all those that rise up against thee to do thee hurt, be as that young man is"; and David, much moved, went up to the chamber over the gate and wept, and as he went thus he said, "O my son Absalom, my son, my son Absalom! would God I had died for thee? O Absalom, my son, my son!" In the bitterness and pathos of that lament, it is not difficult to catch the note of self-approach and condemnation, as if David had said, "My own sins are finding me out."

Great and beautiful and sincere is David's repentance. The immediateness with which forgiveness is announced shows the depth and sincerity of his repentance. He said, "I have sinned against the Lord." The more familiar echo of this repentance we have in that great song of penitence, the Fifty-first Psalm, "Against thee, thee only, have I sinned and done this evil in thy sight." Men have asked, How could David say that? Had he not taken a man's wife, sinned against her, and sinned against her husband whom he had treacherously slain? What then means this, "Against thee, thee only, have I sinned"?

In view of what it teaches about man's duty to man, and the penalties which it pronounces upon injustice and cruelty, and social injustice of every sort, we need have no fear that the Bible underestimates the injury and hurt that man's sin does to his fellowman. Indeed, Christ in his great sermon tells men who come to the altar with a gift, but have some wrong unatoned for in their history, to go first to their brother and be reconciled to him, and then come to the altar of divine forgiveness. But the fact is that all social and moral obligations are founded upon God's holy law. It was just because he had sinned so deeply against Bathsheba and against Uriah that David had sinned so terribly against God, for back of humanity, and in humanity, is God. St. Augustine, in his sermon on the Fifty-first Psalm, answering this question, how David could say, "Against thee only have I sinned," puts it well when he says, "Because thou alone art without sin." However dark his transgression before men, it was darker and more odious in the sight of God who is without sin. True repentance will always be overwhelmed with this thought, and will cry, "Against thee, thee only, have I sinned and done this evil in thy sight."

Because David's repentance was genuine, his forgiveness was immediate and beautiful. The Lamb of God was slain from the foundations of the world, and no measure of time can measure the long preparation of God to forgive man's sin. But the quickness and instantaneousness of that forgiveness, where penitent hearts cry, "I have sinned," is likewise beyond the possibility of human computation. So David, wonderful David, terrible also in this chapter of his life, greatly loving, and greatly sinning, at once the most lovable and most detestable of Old Testament characters, now greatly repenting, comes home to God; and until the whole ransomed Church of Christ has been "saved to sin no more," the story of his fall and repentance and forgiveness will, as David in his prayer asked that it might do, "Teach transgressors thy ways."

Once on the wings of imagination I entered the Holy City, the New Jerusalem, come down from God out of heaven. I saw its twelve flaming gates and its twelve flashing foundations. I wandered by the River of the Water of Life, and rested in the shadows of the Tree of Life, and saw the great company which no man can number, casting down their crowns before the Lamb upon the Throne. The heavenly empire rang with music, the music of the ten thousand times ten thousand, harping with their harps as they stood by the sea of glass mingled with fire; and the song of them that sang the New Song of Moses and the Lamb. But even while I listened, there was silence in heaven for the space of half an hour. The harps stood mute and tuneless, and the voice of the ten thousand times ten thousand was hushed. Then, near the throne, another harper took up his harp; and as he played he began to sing. The music was of heaven; and yet I thought I caught the strain of mortal music too, as if the singer had known and tasted the trials and sorrows and sufferings of life. Yet ever the note was triumphant, as if life were conquering death, as if the dawn were vanquishing the night, as if love were overcoming pain. "Tell me," I said, to one of the glorious Beings who stood about me, "who is that singer? Why are all the other harpers silent? Why are all the angels and archangels, cherubim and seraphim, and all the company of the blood-washed Redeemed now voiceless?" "Mortal," he said, "they are silent and voiceless because they are listening to David, the sweet singer of Israel, the greatest sinner and the greatest saint."

It was the story of the death of a lamb, only a

little innocent lamb, that broke David's heart and showed him how great a sinner he was and brought him to repentance. So it is nothing more, and nothing less, than the story of the death of a Lamb, God's Lamb, the Lamb of God slain from the foundation of the world, that brings men to repentance, shows us how great our sin is, and how great is God's forgiveness. O Lamb of God, that takest away the sins of the world!